PROJECTLAND™
GOES TO THE MOVIES

WHAT THE CRITICS ARE SAYING

"This is the book I wish I had written—fresh, fun, and inspiring. A true game-changer for the profession and a must-have for everyone ready to break free from Groundhog Day."

— Lee R. Lambert, PMP, A Founder of the PMP®, PMI Fellow, PMI Distinguished Contribution Award

"⭐⭐⭐⭐⭐ I give it 6 out of 5 stars! It's a thrilling mix of Hollywood flair and project management genius! Projectland Goes to the Movies delivers a blockbuster performance, turning lessons from the big screen into practical insights that every project manager can actually use even on the smallest project.

Smart, funny, and highly insightful, this one is a rare sequel-worthy business book that proves managing a project can be just as epic as saving the galaxy… or escaping a T-Rex."

— Cornelius Fichtner, PBP, PMP, Host of
The Project Management Podcast

"In my 35 years as a PM, I've never seen such a fun, poignant, and effective way to convey the most crucial lessons to drive project success. While it's particularly resonant for movie buffs, the clear explanations and nicely drawn parallels make it super-useful even if you've never seen ANY of the movies showcased here."

— Michael Hannan, PMP, Co-Author *PMBOK® Guide* 8th Edition; Adjunct Professor, USC Graduate Studies; Industry-Leading Project Portfolio Consultant

"Projectland Goes to the Movies cleverly transforms memorable movie moments into fresh, practical lessons for project professionals. Whether it's leadership insights from a space mission gone wrong or risk management tips from a heist gone right, this book makes learning project management as entertaining as watching your favorite film. Popcorn optional—wisdom guaranteed!"

— Dr. Prasad S. Kodukula, PMP, PgMP, PMI-ACP, DASM, DASSM, BCES, PMI Fellow; *USA Today* Best Selling Author; CEO

"Most people go to the movies simply to enjoy the show and escape their daily routine. Yet in many films, you can actually see how projects are planned and executed. Consider Star Wars and The Empire Strikes Back—the Death Star's construction is a monumental project, and a key stakeholder is not exactly pleased!

In the same spirit, Projectland Goes to the Movies offers many such examples of 'project management in the movies'—an excellent source of insight, inspiration, and creative thinking for anyone involved in leading projects."

— Frank P. Saladis PMP, PMI Fellow

"Every project comes with plot twists, a cast of characters, and moments that swing between Oceans 11 levels of coordination and Top Gun levels of intensity.

This book brings together twenty-two experts who have lived these scenes and distilled the lessons hidden in their favorite films. The result is a collection that proves art and project management mirror each other more closely than we admit, and the insights are as entertaining as they are practical."

— Crystal Richards, Owner of MindsparQ® and author of PMP Exam Prep for Dummies

"As Dirty Harry would say, 'Go ahead, make my day,' and this book will show you exactly how, with strategies that help you conquer challenges, delight stakeholders, and deliver Oscar-winning results.

So grab your popcorn, cue the theme music, and roll the credits on mediocre projects because with these blockbuster strategies, you'll turn every project into a five-star performance."

— Peter 'The Lazy Project Manager' Taylor, Author, Keynote Speaker, Global Project Leadership Executive

"There's something unforgettable about Projectland Goes to the Movies. *The way it draws clean, clever lines between cinema and project management feels both unexpected and exactly right.*

It takes the familiar chaos of movie plots and uses them to illuminate the real-life chaos of running projects, which makes the lessons more engaging, more entertaining, and far easier to remember.

I highly recommend it to any project management professional, whether you are just beginning your journey or a seasoned vet!"

— Laurin Kelly, MPH, PMP, Founder & CEO, Association of Black Women in Project & Program Management (ABWIPPM); CEO & Principal Consultant, Battle Plan

*"*Projectland Goes to the Movies *provides one of the most creative and immediately useful models for putting into clear prose the multiple actions successful project managers must undertake… each chapter offers both useful advice and insightful interpretations of how great cinematic storytelling can shape great lessons when managing for project success."*

— Jeffrey K. Pinto, Ph.D., Andrew Morrow and Elizabeth Lee Black Chair of Technology Management, Penn State University

"The concept for this book is brilliant! I don't know how many times I have watched a movie and thought, 'wow, that's an interesting project' or 'what a great idea for a project manager' or even 'what a bad decision that was.'

Movies are stories about people, and most of our lives are full of stories or interactions with others or adventures and accomplishments. Great projects make great stories, and the movies are full of them, like life. I highly recommend this book!"

— David Pells, Managing Editor, *PM World Journal*

"This book is a highly-readable collection of project management lessons learned from the movies. You'll learn the strategies, shortcuts and straight-up survival tactics that Hollywood accidentally teaches us about leading projects well.

Find out how to set a compelling vision, build trust, navigate egos, manage risk, and keep teams moving when everything goes sideways with insights inspired by films as wide-ranging as Star Wars, Ghostbusters and Raiders of the Lost Ark. And if a project manager had been on the team at Jurassic Park, maybe there wouldn't have been so many sequels…!

Whether you're new to project delivery or have years of experience, Projectland is a fresh, funny and insightful guide to doing work that matters."

— Elizabeth Harrin, APM Fellow, author of Managing Multiple Projects

"Projectland Goes to the Movies brings together brilliant project management minds to reveal what Hollywood has been teaching us all along. With insights drawn from iconic films, this book transforms big-screen lessons into practical strategies for real project success."

— Americo Pinto, PMO Global Alliance Managing Director at PMI

PROJECTLAND™
GOES TO THE MOVIES

22 BLOCKBUSTER STRATEGIES FOR PROJECT SUCCESS

A PROJECT GURU INSIGHT GUIDE

WRITTEN BY THE PROJECT GURUS

EDITED BY
DAWN MAHAN & JERRY MANAS

Copyright © 2026 by Dawn Mahan.
www.PMOtraining.com

Cover and interior design by Covered by Kerry LLC
www.coveredbykerry.com

All rights reserved. Printed in the United States of America.

Projectland® is a registered trademark of PMOtraining, LLC.

PMP® and PMI-ACP® are registered trademarks
of the Project Management Institute (PMI).

CSM® is a registered trademark of Scrum Alliance, Inc.

ITIL® is a registered trademark of AXELOS Limited.

Except as permitted under the United States Copyright Act of 1976, no part of this book may be reproduced in any form or by any electronic or mechanical means, including information storage and retrieval systems, except for brief quotations in critical reviews or articles, without the prior written permission from the publisher.

For permission, email us at info@pmotraining.com with the subject "Copyright Permission Request."

First Edition, January 2026

ISBN (Paperback): 979-8-9904117-3-9
ISBN (Ebook): 979-8-9904117-4-6

Published by Project Guru Press | Summerland Key, FL

CONTENTS

INTRODUCTION 1

ACT I – SETTING THE STAGE: VISION, STRATEGY, & APPROACH . . . 5

CHAPTER 1: Changing the Game 7
How Smart Moves Build Winning Teams and Accelerate Outcomes *(Moneyball)*

CHAPTER 2: Remember, Remember the Fifth of November . . . 15
Making the Impossible Possible *(V for Vendetta)*

CHAPTER 3: Start on the Right Foot 25
How to Kick Off Your Project with Timeless Strategies *(The Great Escape)*

CHAPTER 4: Do You Know What You're Doing? 35
Trusting Your Approach, But Planning for Detours *(Ocean's 11)*

CHAPTER 5: "I've Never Done It, but I've Always Dreamed of It!" . 45
Lessons in Attitude from an Unlucky Italian Accountant *(Fantozzi)*

CHAPTER 6: "I Have a Bad Feeling About This" 55
Risk Management Insights from the Galactic Empire *(Star Wars)*

CHAPTER 7: The Honest Broker and the Rulebreaker 61
Ghostly Secrets for Handling Difficult Executives *(Ghostbusters)*

CHAPTER 8: Fail Fast. Learn Faster. Lead Smarter. 69
How an Agile Astronaut Iterated His Way Home *(The Martian)*

ACT II – DIRECTING THE SHOW: LEADERSHIP & TEAMWORK 77

Chapter 9: Teamwork and Trust in Middle-earth 79
Building Your Project Fellowship *(The Lord of the Rings: Fellowship of the Ring)*

CHAPTER 10: Enough with the Questions Already! 89
    Turning a Collection of Strangers into a Team *(12 Angry Men)*

CHAPTER 11: Lead Like A Warrior 97
    Unlocking Team Power for Breakthrough Success *(Wonder Woman)*

CHAPTER 12: Leadership in the Face of Fear 105
    How Ripley went from Survivor to Strategic Leader *(Aliens)*

CHAPTER 13: In the Line of the Fires 113
    Lava-Hot Lessons on Conflict and Crisis Leadership *(The Fires)*

CHAPTER 14: "Let's Work the Problem, People" 121
    How to Respond When Everything Seems Lost *(Apollo 13)*

CHAPTER 15: Smoke Out 'Dem Deadly Snakes 129
    Building Trust & Sidestepping Sabotage *(The Italian Job)*

CHAPTER 16: Navigating Egos & Cultures 137
    A Wild Ride from the Saddle of Vendor Delivery *(The Man from Snowy River)*

ACT III – HERDING CATS: A PROJECTLAND PRODUCTION 149

CHAPTER 17: Check Your Ego at the Door 151
    Change Enablement in High-Powered Teams *(The Greatest Night in Pop)*

CHAPTER 18: "I'm Making This Up As I Go" 161
    Leading on Purpose *(Raiders of the Lost Ark)*

CHAPTER 19: Spared No Expense 169
    Managing Your Sponsor Without Getting Eaten *(Jurassic Park)*

CHAPTER 20: The Power of Authentic Relationships 179
    Rocking Stakeholder Engagement *(School of Rock)*

CHAPTER 21: Mastering the Art of Negotiation 187
    Lessons in Adapting, Listening, and Leverage *(Cash Out)*

CHAPTER 22: Check Your Six!................ 197
    Maintaining Team Performance Under Pressure *(Top Gun)*

ACKNOWLEDGEMENTS 205
SPECIAL NOTE FROM THE EDITORS 207
CONTINUE YOUR PROJECTLAND JOURNEY! 209
ENDNOTES......................... 211

WHAT IS A PROJECT GURU INSIGHT GUIDE?

OUR PROJECT GURU INSIGHT GUIDES ARE CONCISE, PRACTICAL resources crafted for ambitious professionals who want real-world wisdom that works.

These guides are designed to be:

- Expert-driven *(featuring insights from seasoned project leaders)*
- Realistic *(based on hands-on experience running projects in diverse industries)*
- Actionable *(offering tips and strategies you can use immediately)*
- Relatable *(presented in a clear, straightforward style without unnecessary jargon)*
- Fun *(we don't do boring—our guides make learning and doing project management as engaging and enjoyable as possible)*

With a *Project Guru Insight Guide* in hand, you gain access to tested advice and lessons from people who've been in the trenches—navigating challenges, driving results, and leading successful projects every day.

Sometimes, insights spring from surprising places—history, fables, leadership stories, new technologies, and more—always chosen for their practical, expert-driven value. No theoretical models here—just trusted guidance to help you sharpen your skills, overcome obstacles, and elevate your projects to success with confidence and less stress.

This is the first in a growing series of Insight Guides aimed at delivering practical knowledge that empowers project professionals at all levels.

For every project player ready to face the plot twists, drama, and cliffhangers in Projectland and make their story a success.

PROJECTLAND

PROJECTLAND [NOUN PROJ-EKT-LAND]

1. A concept to convey that projects are like a different world with different roles and rules.

2. Consider Projectland a place with a capital P like Pluto, Poland, Pennsylvania, and Philadelphia. Each have their own terrain, challenges, and opportunities. When traveling to a new place for the first time, it's best to prepare.

ORIGIN

Dawn Mahan coined the term projectland first without the Capital P prior to 2018, when she blurted it out during a live, corporate training session. In 2020, passionate Book Insider VIPs insisted it be capitalized like a real place.

She applied for the trademark in 2022, and it was officially registered for training and workshops in 2024, so we began using the ® symbol. She subsequently applied for Projectland to be trademarked for e-books and printed books, as well. This is why we currently have the TM in certain places, pending official approval. So if you were wondering why we appear to be having a trademark identity crisis, now you know, and it's because we are. In fact, it's driving Dawn nuts that it doesn't match everywhere.

Because it's really annoying to do so, we will not continue to show the trademark every time we mention Projectland in the book. The Projectland image above was developed in 2023 by Beth Montgomery in collaboration with Jerry Manas and Dawn Mahan. We all hope you like it, and that the concept helps you to embrace and conquer this wild world.

"The whole of life is just like watching a film. Only it's as though you always get in ten minutes after the big picture has started, and no-one will tell you the plot, so you have to work it out all yourself from the clues."

— Sir Terry Pratchett, *Moving Pictures*

CONTRIBUTING AUTHORS & THEIR FEATURED FILMS

In Order of Appearance

GRAYSON AND LAURA BARNARD	MONEYBALL *(2011)*
RUTH PEARCE	V FOR VENDETTA *(2005)*
DR. MARK KOZAK-HOLLAND	THE GREAT ESCAPE *(1963)*
JUSTUS AIYELA	OCEANS 11 *(2001)*
BRUNO MORGANTE	FANTOZZI *(1975)*
JERRY MANAS	STAR WARS *(1980)*
CHRIS CLEWS	GHOSTBUSTERS *(1984)*
JAMES EVANS	THE MARTIAN *(2015)*
RACHEL MUSSELL AND MICHAEL SCHAFER	THE LORD OF THE RINGS: FELLOWSHIP OF THE RING *(2001)*
JOE PUSZ	12 ANGRY MEN *(1957)*
MARIE VILLEGAS	WONDER WOMAN *(2017)*

Tanya Boyd	Aliens *(1986)*
Dr. Haukur Ingi Jónasson	The Fires *(2025)*
Dr. Mike Clayton	Apollo 13 *(1995)*
Dawn Mahan	The Italian Job *(2003)*
Rosalind Guy	The Man from Snowy River *(1982)*
Rosalin Walcott	The Greatest Night in Pop *(2024)*
Michael Schafer	Raiders of the Lost Ark *(1981)*
Jesse Middaugh	Jurassic Park *(1993)*
Rachel Mussell	School of Rock *(2003)*
John Salah	Cash Out *(2024)*
Dave Lozinger	Top Gun *(1986)*

INTRODUCTION

WELCOME TO THE ONLY PROJECT MANAGEMENT BOOK INSPIRED by a blockbuster lineup of movies, from the courtroom to capers to otherworldly adventures.

If you think movie critics are harsh, it's even harder to earn rave reviews from project stakeholders. You can't please everyone, and some people are never satisfied.

Let's face it, most projects fail because the people aren't set up for success.

Systems don't get projects done. Software doesn't get projects done. Process doesn't get projects done. Even planning with the help of Artificial Intelligence won't get projects done.

Because, ultimately, none of it means anything without people.

Project people *(that's everyone involved in project success—sponsors, steering teams, project managers, team members, regardless of your title)* need to be able to communicate well; to have both a planful and an adaptive mindset; to know when to push forward and when to be prudent.

We believe project success principles should be easy—and fun—to learn and apply. So we thought: what better way to do that than to share project insights from the world of cinema? After all, movies are real life, exaggerated.

With this in mind, we came up with an epiphany: Why not gather experts from Projectland *(that's the term Dawn coined for the world of projects)* who are also film buffs, and ask them to write a chapter sharing the most valuable project lessons from their favorite movie?

And that's exactly what we did.

In these pages you will find 22 chapters, each one highlighting a different film. This book is for project managers—official or unofficial—sponsors, department heads, and team members. If you lead, fund, or participate in projects and love movies, you're in for a treat!

Gain crucial insights through the lens of cinema, including:

- Self-confidence from *Oceans 11*
- Staying on track from *Raiders of the Lost Ark*
- Leading through fear from *Aliens*
- Teamwork and trust from *Lord of the Rings*
- Problem-solving strategies from *Apollo 13*
- Performing under pressure from *Top Gun*
- … and more film favorites, from *Moneyball* to *V for Vendetta*!

Our story is organized into three acts:

- Act I – **Setting the Stage:** Vision, Strategy, & Approach
- Act II – **Directing the Show:** Leadership & Teamwork
- Act III – **Herding Cats:** A Projectland Production

Each chapter delivers not only a film's summary and the pivotal scene, but also hands-on project tips, expert insights, and a personal connection to make every lesson memorable.

We hope you find this blend of project wisdom and movie magic both entertaining and actionable… and maybe discover new films for your watchlist!

For bonus resources including ideas for how to use this book to engage your project people, the IMDb links to view movie trailers, and more, visit ProjectGuruPress.com/MovieBook.

Grab your popcorn—project success is about to get much more entertaining. Read on to master your next project—Hollywood style. Lights, camera…action!

Your fellow movie-loving project people,
Dawn and Jerry

PS: As with every great movie production, rest assured—no animals-were harmed in the making of this book.

SHAPING A CLEAR VISION AND STRATEGY SETS A STRONG FOUNDATION FOR ANY PROJECT.

GAIN PRACTICAL INSIGHTS INTO EFFECTIVE PLANNING, ADAPTABLE THINKING, AND EMBRACING CALCULATED RISKS TO PREPARE FOR SUCCESS FROM THE START.

SETTING THE STAGE
VISION, STRATEGY, & APPROACH

ACT I

CHAPTER 1

CHANGING THE GAME

How smart moves build winning teams and accelerate outcomes *(Moneyball)*

Moneyball (2011)
Logline: "Oakland A's general manager Billy Beane attempts to assemble a competitive team on a limited budget by using data-driven player evaluation techniques that defy traditional scouting."[1]

SETTING THE SCENE

BILLY BEANE *(BRAD PITT)* TAKES OVER AS THE NEW GENERAL Manager for the Oakland Athletics in the 2002 season. He immediately faces countless challenges in his new role—a tiny budget, losing top players to other teams, and resistance from old school baseball coaches and scouts who think success comes from swagger, not stats.

The Oakland A's need to rebuild their team after losing several star players, but they don't have the budget to replace them using traditional scouting methods or high dollar contracts. Billy realizes he'll need a completely different approach. He can't win by outspending the big budget teams, so he has to win by outthinking them. And that's where things get interesting.

Billy meets Peter Brand *(Jonah Hill)*, a young economics graduate who explains the concept of using analytics and different metrics to find undervalued players. Instead of looking at batting averages, body types, or *"star power,"* Billy and Peter look at one key metric: whether a player can get on base. Peter explains, *"People who run ball clubs, they think in terms of buying players. Your goal shouldn't be to buy players. Your goal should be to buy wins. And in order to buy wins, you need to buy runs."*

This new, data-driven approach is a fundamental shift from the traditional methods of scouting and team building. It challenges the old school mindset that is heavily based on gut instinct, player reputation, and even what the girlfriends of the players look like. As a result, scouts, coaches, and the media criticize Billy and Peter. When the pressure is on, Billy teaches us what it looks like to:

- Think creatively when you have a limited budget but big goals.
- Stay grounded in your strategy, even when no one else believes in it yet.
- Focus on progress metrics that actually move you toward your goals—like getting on base leads to runs, and runs lead to wins.

LAURA'S PERSPECTIVE

This is where the movie starts to mirror the challenges I see with project teams every day. They're often stuck in old patterns—prioritizing activity over impact, or appearances over results. They focus on implementing flashy tools before addressing the core process challenges that are keeping them stuck. But once you shift to an outcome-first mindset, just like Billy did, everything changes.

> **HOT TAKE:** In business and baseball, if you want to win, stop chasing what looks good and start focusing on what gets results.

🍿 THE MOVIE MOMENT

In one of the most important scenes of *Moneyball*, Billy Beane sits in a room surrounded by his old-school baseball scouts. They're discussing potential players to fill gaps after the loss of three of their star players. But the scouts are focused on superficial measures of success like player confidence and swagger, how they swing the bat, and if they are popular. The scouts say, *"We're trying to solve the problem here, Billy."*

Billy finally snaps and slams his fists on the table in frustration.

"Not like this. You're not even looking at the problem."

Billy explains that their traditional focus is keeping them from solving the root problem. This isn't about finding players who look the part. It's about building a team that can win games.

He explains that the secret to their success is shifting from buying players to buying wins. And to get wins, you need runs. To get runs, you need guys who get on base. It's not flashy, it's against the norm, but it works.

Billy's strategy to shift from traditional team building to creating a team based on this one metric seems reckless to his old school management team, but Billy is willing to risk everything to change the game. Everyone thinks he's crazy, but he sticks with it. And the team goes from chasing stars to chasing wins, one base at a time.

And it works. The A's go on a historic 20-game winning streak, breaking the American League record, and make the playoffs with a team full of *"misfits"* the scouts wrote off. They didn't have the biggest names or the flashiest stats, but they had the one thing that mattered: players who could consistently get on base. The result? Wins. This wasn't just a feel-good theory. It was a winning strategy. One that changed the way teams think about baseball forever.

"ACTION!!!" PROJECTLAND SUCCESS TIPS

In baseball, the focus was on outputs like how good a player looked, their batting average, or whether they could hit home runs. But Billy realized that those stats didn't always translate into wins. What mattered more was whether a player could consistently get on base. Getting on base leads to runs and runs win games. That's what happens when you focus on outcomes instead of outputs.

In business, teams often chase metrics like how busy people are, or if the project will be on time and on budget. But just like in baseball, those metrics don't really define success. What wins the game in baseball and in business, is whether you are achieving the intended goals. In baseball, it's getting on base, in business, it's delivering measurable impact.

LAURA'S PERSPECTIVE

I've worked with thousands of project and PMO professionals, and I've seen this same pattern play out again and again: when teams value activity—like checking boxes or only hitting traditional time, scope, and budget metrics—they lose sight of what really drives success. The shift from outputs to outcomes is the game changer. Just like Billy stopped chasing star players and focused instead on getting on base, the most successful teams stop chasing tasks and instead focus on achieving measurable business results. When everyone is aligned on what winning really means, you don't have to push against resistance to get to the goal. The team moves together in the same direction, one base at a time.

Moneyball is based on a true story, and you too can find a way to win against the odds in your version of Projectland.

Start with the real problem. Strategic success isn't about tracking inputs or perfecting outputs; it's about solving the right problem to achieve meaningful outcomes.

When resources are limited *(as they usually are)*, align your team on outcomes. That focus unlocks creative solutions to drive project success.

Winning starts with small measurable progress, like simply getting on base.

Stay grounded in your strategy even when others push back. You must believe if you want them to believe.

If you want your team to believe in their ability to succeed so that they give their all, you have to believe in them first.

Incremental, intentional action beats flashy, uncoordinated effort every time.

None of this is theory. We've seen how leaders can keep everyone on the team focused on outcomes to help the team win, whether on a project team or in a dugout filled with baseball players.

📣 DIRECTOR'S COMMENTS

LAURA'S PERSPECTIVE

Grayson and I have watched *Moneyball* together countless times. We love baseball and quality time snuggled up on the couch. While most of our movie nights are for fun, anything involving baseball is serious business in our house.

From the very first time we watched the movie together, he noticed something powerful: Billy had to stay grounded in his vision and bring the scouts and manager through the change process even when they didn't believe in his approach. Project managers are often in situations where they must keep everyone aligned on the goals, even when there are so many distractions and reasons teams can spin on the wrong things.

GRAYSON'S PERSPECTIVE

This movie moment really connects to me personally. My business career began as I watched my mother help a nonprofit discuss their business strategy. Sitting at that table, witnessing transformation happen right in front of my eyes, she took the nonprofit leaders on a journey from feeling stuck and overwhelmed with how much they needed to do, to finding clarity and purpose by answering three questions:

- What are we doing?
- Why are we doing it?
- What does success look like?

Once they understood the answer to those three questions, their entire approach changed. They were now able to see a new way to solve the problem. That moment unlocked something for me. I took seven pages of notes on my phone. Not because I had to, but because I needed to remember as much as possible about the mindset shift and transformation happening in front of me. Instead of getting overwhelmed by all of the things they didn't know, I learned that asking these three simple questions allowed the nonprofit to get unstuck and have clarity on what mattered most. They were ready to move toward their mission-critical goals.

In baseball, it's easy to focus on how things look instead of what actually gets results. I used to care a lot about my batting stats—too much in fact. I'll admit it, I hated bunting. It almost always meant I was going to be an easy out, and to be honest, it didn't look great on paper. No one's impressed by a bunt in the stat line. But then I started to really understand *the why* behind it. A bunt isn't flashy or fun, but if it moves the runner into scoring position, it changes the game. It's not about personal stats; it's about helping the team win.

Once that clicked for me, I started practicing bunting on purpose. Not just to check the box, but to perfect the art of bunting so I could use it when the game was on the line. That mindset-shift from *"How does this make me look?"* to *"How does this help us move forward?"* completely changed how I played the game. And now that I've worked in business, I see the same thing happening with teams. People chase the big, flashy projects or try to look busy, but if what you're doing doesn't help you score runs, it's just noise. I've seen this play out at school and at internships that have helped me learn more about the real business world. Whether it's baseball or business, the real question is: are you getting your team to the next base?

🎬 REALITY SHOW: WHEN LIFE IMITATES ART

It's the bottom of the final inning in our league's championship game. We were the home team, down by three runs, and running out of chances. Two walks and a passed ball gave us a shot. The batter before me ripped a double, and suddenly we're down by one.

I step up to the plate with the weight of the world on my shoulders and my dad on my mind. He had passed away only four months before. My confidence just isn't the same without him standing at the end of the fence cheering me on.

I stand in the box, a cold streak of hitless attempts throughout the season, and here I am with the tying run on second in the last inning of the championship game. My father taught me everything I know about baseball whether on the field, rummaging through baseball cards, or from behind home plate as we cheered on our favorite team. This moment is for him.

The first two pitches came and went. Ball one. Ball two. I'm thinking about every moment I spent practicing with my father, every swing of the bat I took to progress to this moment. The pitcher begins his wind-up. A fastball, right down the middle. This is my pitch. Smack. Line drive over the shortstop's head. Runner scores. Game tied. I make it to second base.

My coach gives me the steal sign. I take my lead. Eyes locked on the pitcher's front leg. I spent countless hours practicing stealing with my dad. Every time he would do a funky windup and try to pick me off. I'd laugh so uncontrollably as he swung his leg around in the air that I couldn't breathe.

Next thing I know, I'm stealing third. SAFE.

I'm so close to home. Last ninety feet of the game. I hear the bat crack and someone yells, ***"Run!"*** Maybe it was my coach, maybe it was my team, but in my heart, I knew that voice. It was my dad. He was here.

To slide into home plate, I must get through the largest catcher I'd ever faced. The ball whizzes past me as I see the catcher get ready to make the tag. But I'm sliding through his legs and my foot touches home plate. Dirt flies into the air creating a cloud covering home.

We both freeze and look up at the umpire. ***"SAFE!"***

We did it! We won. I jump up from the plate, throw my helmet to the ground and run straight toward my coach who's about 5 feet off the ground, screaming. I jump into his arms as he says, ***"Grayson, your dad was here with us the whole time!"***

We didn't win with one big swing. It happened one base at a time. One decision at a time. One moment of confidence at a time. That's what leadership is. You don't need a home run to win. You just need to keep moving forward and help your team do the same.

LAURA'S PERSPECTIVE

Watching Grayson throughout this particular baseball season was both heartbreaking and inspiring. I've seen senior leaders freeze at high-stakes moments because they're waiting for the perfect plan. But what Grayson did here is exactly what project leaders need to do: see the opportunity in front of them and act, even when the outcome isn't guaranteed.

Whether it's a baseball game or a big project, you don't need the perfect conditions to achieve success. You just need to know how to move steadily toward your goals, base by base.

🎬 "IT'S A WRAP!"

The next time you are on a project with time and budget constraints *(like all of them)*, don't just follow the usual playbook. Challenge the status quo. Ask why the work matters. What's the real business problem you're solving?

Then, align your team around that purpose. Not the process, not the paperwork, but the outcome. Remember that it's not about following the old school process simply because you've ***"always done it that way"*** or tying your success to how fancy your templates and tools might be. It's all about getting on base so that you can win games.

Whether you're rebuilding a team or driving strategic change, real leadership is about making visible progress, one base at a time.

🎬 PRESENTED BY...

GRAYSON BARNARD

Grayson is a high school senior dual-enrolled in college, where he's pursuing his passions in business and computer science with the goal of making a positive impact on the world. Since 8th grade, he has also worked in his mom's company, PMO Strategies, gaining hands-on experience in strategy delivery and project leadership. Grayson has also been an active volunteer with the nonprofit Project Management for Change since its very first Project Management Day of Service® event in 2015, contributing his time to help solve real-world problems for mission-driven nonprofit organizations. He also started playing baseball officially when he was three years old but turned every household object into a bat or a ball the day he turned one.

LAURA BARNARD

For nearly three decades, Laura has spearheaded efforts to unleash the power of effective project management to help organizations rapidly achieve higher returns on investment for their strategic goals. Her company's groundbreaking *IMPACT Engine System* empowers organizations to drive transformational outcomes aligned to their vision with unprecedented speed and measurable business IMPACT. You can read more about this system in her book, *The IMPACT Engine: Accelerating Strategy Delivery for PMO and Transformation Leaders*.

Originally from the Washington, D.C., area, Laura and Grayson now reside in South Florida with Kurt—who not only resembles a superhero but actually was one in the Army.

CHAPTER 2

REMEMBER, REMEMBER THE FIFTH OF NOVEMBER

Making the Impossible Possible *(V for Vendetta)*

V for Vendetta
Logline: "In a future British dystopian society, a shadowy freedom fighter, known only by the alias of 'V', plots to overthrow the tyrannical government - with the help of a young woman."[2]

SETTING THE SCENE

ONE OF MY EARLIEST ENCOUNTERS WITH PROJECT MANAGEment—although I did not know it at the time—was Bonfire Night in the village in the United Kingdom where I grew up. Each year on November 5th, the local large historic house in the village – owned by the same family for generations - would put on fireworks, a bonfire and provide food and drink for the community. On a clear night they could get 200-400 people. On wet weather days not so many. Although everyone looked forward to this annual event, to me, as a young girl, it was all normal. We showed up, everything was provided for the guests, we had fun, we went home. The bonfire was always HUGE, and the traditional food tasty. Although the fireworks were hardly the Macy's July 4th extravaganza, they were fun.

For those unfamiliar with Bonfire Night and Guy Fawkes, this is one of our British traditions—to commemorate the day Guy Fawkes and his Catholic co-conspirators were foiled in their attempt to blow up the House of Lords *(part of the Houses of Parliament)* in London. Their aim was to assassinate the king and much of the Protestant government and restore a Catholic monarch to the throne. The plot failed, and the event has been remembered annually with bonfires and fireworks.

Years later as an adult, when organizing a similar but smaller scale event, I realized the amount of planning that must have gone into that annual community event—let alone the original plot! And I thought about all the things that can go wrong along the way. The weather is only one of them.

When *V for Vendetta* came out, I was delighted. It blended my love of movies with that age-old *"good overcomes evil"* theme, since the people aimed to take back their rights. And it was all planned and orchestrated by one man—the project manager known as V.

V for Vendetta is set in a grim future, where a fascist regime rules Britain with an iron fist. The protagonist, V, is a mysterious, highly intelligent freedom fighter who wears a Guy Fawkes mask. V's mission is to dismantle the oppressive government by inspiring the masses—the ordinary people—to rise and reclaim their autonomy. As he says when he is urging people to join him, *"People shouldn't be afraid of their government. Governments should be afraid of their people."*

Among my favorite clips is the pivotal *"Domino Scene,"* where V's months of careful planning come together in a spectacular chain reaction. It's a masterclass in strategic thinking, vision, and execution—all hallmarks of successful project management.

> **HOT TAKE:** Having a clear vision, a well thought out plan, and an adaptive, engaged team will inspire magnificent outcomes, even when it seems impossible.

 THE MOVIE MOMENT

THE DOMINO SCENE

By this point in the movie, we have already seen that V is meticulous. He leaves nothing to chance.

In this scene, V meticulously sets up thousands of black and red dominoes in a dramatic visual representation of his plans. Each piece seems to represent a person, an event, or a strategic move. As he builds this domino cascade, the scene intercuts with key characters and actions in motion: citizens receiving Guy Fawkes masks, the government scrambling to regain control, and the crescendo of a revolution beginning to unfold.

At a key point, when one of the main characters, played by the incomparable Stephen Rea, says, *"All V has to do is keep his word . . . and then . . ."* V topples the first domino.

All his tasks are in place, the chain of events is almost complete, and his project is nearing its conclusion.

This moment symbolizes the culmination of V's long-term strategy, where individual efforts combine to create a larger, unstoppable movement. It's a vivid reminder of how every small step in a project can lead to monumental outcomes.

"ACTION!!!" PROJECTLAND SUCCESS TIPS

From *V for Vendetta*, we can extract many lessons for project managers. Here are five of my favorites:

HAVE A CLEAR VISION

V is clear and relentless in his pursuit of his overarching vision—freedom for the people—which guides every decision he makes. Similarly, project managers need a clear vision that inspires their teams and stakeholders. Even when distractions arise, time and again he steers himself back to his goal. No scope creep in this project!

One of the key questions to ask on big projects—especially in response to a scope change request—is, *"How does this align with the overall purpose and goals of the project?"* This helps us to avoid *"tack-on"* changes being proposed opportunistically by people who have an agenda separate from the project mandate.

PLAN STRATEGICALLY, BE METHODICAL

V hardly ever acts impulsively. He carefully aligns each domino *(or task)*, ensuring everything is in place for a smooth execution. Indeed, when he does go outside of his careful plan there are dangerous consequences. Only after careful weighing of his actions and potential consequences does he do something that was not part of the original plan.

Break down your projects into manageable steps, aligning them with your end goal. And do your best to avoid distractions.

One of the challenges with amazing teams is that they tend to be innovative. It is all too easy for someone to come up with a *"great new way"* to do something. If this is the case for your team, create a process for evaluating new ideas to assess whether they merit incorporation into the plan. In one organization I led projects for, we had a three-stage process that asked the following questions:

- How is it measurably better than the original approach?
- Who does it serve most?
- What do we give up if we do or don't adopt the new idea?

This allowed the team to continue to be creative, while also ensuring that we were methodical and didn't deviate accidentally from our plan.

EMPOWER OTHERS

V doesn't work alone; he inspires ordinary people to act by saying out loud and in public what many are already thinking but feel powerless to do anything about.

Two of my favorite themes in the movie are collaboration and inspiration. Project managers who foster a sense of ownership and collaboration within their teams see better results; people go above and beyond and sometimes make what seems impossible happen!

One thing to keep in mind in Project land is that team members are often brought together from across departments for a project and their current job title doesn't matter anymore. In my projects, I discovered that project team members brought helpful and relevant experience from other dimensions of their life and work experience. So, we always had an *"if you see something, say something"* approach.

We created a positive environment, instilling a *"yes, and"* approach *(an improv acting tool that encourages building upon what the previous person said)*. This purposefully avoided situations where people might have felt criticized or undermined. Anyone could offer an idea based on their experiences. This also helped us to avoid *"expert syndrome,"* where people do things because the expert says so. After all, every project is unique, so no one can really be an expert until the project is over.

PREPARE TO PIVOT

V anticipates obstacles and adjusts his plans as needed. But he can't foresee every chance encounter or setback and must sometimes adjust in the moment. Most of his tasks are well defined and planned, but every so often there is a curve ball from one of the other characters.

Be prepared to pivot when things don't go as planned. Part of our planning process was always to consider *"what happens if things don't go as planned?"* This is risk assessment and contingency planning, and it's critical. We cannot assume that things will go as we expect. While we don't want to become mired in *"what ifs,"* we do want to make sure we have a plan for how we will adapt and pivot when *(not if)* the need arises. Our pre-planned approaches will not solve everything, but the process of considering alternatives makes us more attentive, more observant, and more nimble.

SYMBOLISM AND COMMUNICATION MATTER

The Guy Fawkes mask became a unifying symbol.

In project management, clear, symbolic communication can motivate teams and align stakeholders. This can be as simple as a team name, recognition or rewards, or promoting team successes, but also implies a team persona. Teams want and need a clear identity that aligns with their purpose.

A team that is not treated as a reputable unit often feels unseen or unappreciated. Lack of recognition is not just about missing a few pats on the back, it is about feeling that everyone knows who to go to for their needs and when. When teams feel that they are not the go-to for anything, they feel disengaged.

Having a clear team identity brings the team together and makes it easier for other teams to recognize who they are and what they do. On one team that was building the central hub that all the satellite systems would connect to, we declared that we were like the sun, and all the other teams were planets. This may sound a bit grandiose, but it did the trick. Everyone better understood the importance of our team's work, and we gained status and recognition that helped reinvigorate the team. We did not, however, wear Guy Fawkes masks to identify the group.

📣 DIRECTOR'S COMMENTS

I love the movie because it's a brilliant representation of how visionary leadership, strategic planning, and teamwork can lead to great change. On a personal level, it reminds me of the power of persistence and preparation. It emphasizes the importance of staying on task and, when faced with inevitable distractions, weighing them and then minimizing their impact.

When I first started managing large projects, I often felt overwhelmed by the scope of work. Another thing that overwhelmed me was stakeholders changing their minds about what they want.

Watching V set up his dominoes reinforced the importance of taking it one step at a time, trusting that each piece contributes to the larger picture. His patient and meticulous focus on his goal reminds me to respectfully challenge stakeholders who start adding to the wish list.

While we need to be flexible in projects and open to the possibility that requirements will evolve, we also need to avoid being reactive. To do this we need a rigorous process for evaluating and prioritizing new requirements.

To avoid adding unnecessary project dominoes that are either superfluous, interrupt the flow, or knock over the other dominoes prematurely, we must always refer back to the project purpose and ask how the extra domino enhances and supports that purpose.

Another part of the movie that is less obvious is V's deep understanding of how people tick. He has an extraordinary capacity to understand what people are thinking and how they will act. This level of emotional intelligence and empathy is another trait effective project managers share. It is difficult to pivot and adapt to the unexpected if you don't understand what matters to others. By taking time to appreciate the values and thought processes of his *"team,"* V is able to reduce the number of unexpected events.

🎥 REALITY SHOW: WHEN LIFE IMITATES ART

A few years ago, I was the program manager for part of an enterprise-wide technology implementation. We were one of multiple teams working on different aspects of the program, and there was also a vendor team with which we were collaborating.

At first, the task of taking over the team with all the threads of communication and influence felt insurmountable—there were so many departments, stakeholders, and moving parts! But by channeling V's strategic mindset, we broke the project into the following *"dominoes"*:

Identify key goals (the vision). At the heart of the overall program was a better experience for customers who want to effectively manage their finances through multiple stages of life.

Map out individual tasks and dependencies. This is not something we could do once. We had to reevaluate, adjust and consider both the expected and unknown risks. It became important to inspire and engage the team on a regular basis, just as V does by addressing the people's fears and boosting their confidence by sending them masks.

Align team members with their strengths and not just their roles—and have clear values. One of the things that shows up in *V for Vendetta* is V's ability to get the other players not just to be true to their roles but also to their strengths and values. In our team we had a business analyst who had a top strength of humor. He was often seen as flippant and other members of the team accused him of not taking his role seriously. However, once we found an outlet for his humor that others could appreciate – he introduced something fun at the daily stand up – his worth as a business analyst became much more apparent. He valued the camaraderie that comes from shared fun and helped us build a more engaged and inclusive team.

Establish checkpoints to assess progress and pivot when needed. Throughout the movie V is checking where he is in the plan and handling obstacles as they arise. This is the nature of Projectland, and we certainly needed to pivot while staying true to our goal too.

Empower others via a unifying identity. Just as V creates an identity that others can get behind and that offers them the protection of some anonymity, so project managers and their teams can create identities that help them stand as one unit and deliver a consistent message. That way it is not a team member or the project manager delivering bad news, it is the team.

Soon after I became the program manager of a large team spread across multiple international locations, I realized the team was having an identity crisis. Our primary location in the US was in the basement of the building. The team was out of sight and often out of mind. They felt that many design and strategic decisions were being made without consulting them, and they were being forced to live with—and code around—the technical consequences of these decisions.

To challenge the positioning of the team as the *"afterthought,"* we created a catchy name for the team and an insignia. We even had a mascot—a cuddly sheep toy that also doubled as a comforter when things got stressful!

To get our point across, we decided to explain *(as mentioned earlier)* that we were like the sun at the center of the enterprise program universe. One night when almost everyone in the office had gone home, three of us printed our sun and planet insignia and pinned it up all over the offices where the other teams were sitting. We added that insignia to our email signatures, which was a visual queue reminding people to include us before decisions were made and not afterwards.

At the time I was unsure how that would be received—or whether it would make any difference. Fortunately, it worked wonders. To this day

I have a large poster of that insignia. I realize now that it was like our Guy Fawkes mask. It empowered the team and sent a clear message to the powers that be—this team mattered.

Throughout my tenure as program manager there were moments when unforeseen challenges felt like someone had bumped into the dominoes too early. But the plan's structure, the team members' collaboration and creativity, and the way we played to our individual strengths, allowed us to recover and keep moving forward. By the end, not only was the team perceived as a lynchpin in the overall program, but our work practices also created a ripple effect of improved collaboration and morale across the company.

🎬 "IT'S A WRAP!"

As project managers, we often face complex, high-stakes challenges. The lessons from *V for Vendetta* remind us to think big, plan strategically, and inspire others to join us on the journey. It also reminds us that a large project may take a long time from inception to completion and that to do it right, there are no shortcuts. Slow and steady, thoughtful and deliberate, intentional and sensitive to others, gets the project done!

Next time you're managing a project, remember V's dominoes. Every task, every person, and every decision is a critical piece of the bigger picture. By aligning them carefully, you can create a chain reaction that leads to extraordinary outcomes.

🎬 PRESENTED BY...

RUTH PEARCE, JD, PCC, PMP

Ruth Pearce is an international speaker, coach and trainer in leadership and workplace mental health, as well as a character strength, team building and leadership expert. For 25 years she was a passionate project management leader, before turning her attention to bringing the leader out in all of us.

Her first book, *Be a Project Motivator*, was described by Dr. Ryan Niemiec of the VIA Institute on Character as the first of its kind. She is the author of *Be Hopeful, Be Strong, Be Brave, Be Curious* which helps coaches and coaching clients understand how coaching works. Ruth is also the creator of five LinkedIn Learning Courses for project managers. As a professional speaker and educator, she inspires individuals and organizations to embrace the power of behavioral science and leadership excellence, to listen with intention and speak with purpose.

When not speaking or coaching, you may find Ruth playing with her two dogs Luka & Misha, two rabbits BunnyPenny and Dylan, or tending her beehive. Next, she plans to add chickens and goats to her menagerie. A love of nature, music – and movies – keeps her grounded, focused and persistent!

To learn more about Ruth's work, visit her website at: https://www.aleverlongenough.org/

CHAPTER 3

START ON THE RIGHT FOOT

How to Kick Off Your Project with Timeless Strategies *(The Great Escape)*

The Great Escape (1963)
Logline: "Allied officers in a German prisoner of war camp during World War II make a daring plan for a mass escape by hundreds of their men, hoping to draw German personnel and resources away from combat operations."[3]

SETTING THE SCENE

IN 1963, PAUL BRICKHILL'S BOOK WAS TURNED INTO A MOVIE that became a vast, multi-star war epic and a blockbuster for the year. It is a story of extraordinary courage in the face of life-threatening odds and represents the people who fought and died for their countries. Today it still is one of the most popular movies of all time, and probably one of the best World War II movies ever made. It is a global phenomenon. In the United Kingdom, it's an iconic movie, on TV almost every single Christmas, and it is so cemented into the popular culture that the majority of school children will have seen it.

If you haven't seen it, don't worry. Let's set the scene with what you need to know.

Roger Bartlett *(played by Richard Attenborough)* was captured by the Gestapo in Prague and placed into a Prisoner of War *(POW)* camp. He escaped, was on the run for 7 months, and then retrieved by the Luftwaffe *(the German air force)*. The Luftwaffe were at odds with the Gestapo—thus, he was spared execution but was once again a prisoner. On arriving at the Luftwaffe's POW camp, he is quickly appointed as **"the Big X"** or Chief Escape Officer.

However, the Luftwaffe Camp Commandant cautions the Senior Allied Officer that the camp has been set up to be escape proof:

Colonel von Luger: *"It [the camp] has been built to incorporate all we have learned from security measures. We have in effect put all our rotten eggs in one basket. And we intend to watch this basket carefully."*

This specific scene highlights how Stalag Luft III, was built for the express purpose of housing many of the Luftwaffe's most troublesome captured Allied airmen. Not only was this a prison, but the Luftwaffe personnel were highly trained escape prevention specialists that would shut down anything that resembled a project to enable an escape.

> **HOT TAKE:** Projects can be under pressure from day one, scrutinized, questioned, and targeted for early shutdown. Set your project up for success with an outstanding kickoff meeting and extensive planning.

🍿 THE MOVIE MOMENT

Bartlett *(the Big X)* meets the Escape Committee for the first time to lay out his vision for the escape.

```
Bartlett: Gentlemen, no doubt you've heard the
immortal words of our new commandant: devote your
energies to things other than escape and sit out the
war as comfortably as possible.

Sedgwick: [derisively] Ha!

Bartlett: Well, that's exactly what we're going to
do. We're going to devote our energies to sports
and gardening, all the cultural pursuits as far
as they're concerned. In fact, we're going to put
the goons to sleep. Meanwhile, we dig. Now, even a
superficial look at the compound shows us that Huts
104 and 5 are closest to the woods. The first tunnel
goes out from 105, directly east under the vorlager,
the cooler, and the wire.

Willie: But that's over three hundred feet, Roger!
```

Bartlett: Did you make a survey, Dennis?

Cavendish: Only a temporary one, sir. I make it just over three hundred and thirty-five feet.

Bartlett: Let me know when you've got an exact one. Willie, this time we'll dig straight down thirty feet before we go horizontal. That'll rule out any question of sound detection or probing.

We can see from how this *"project kickoff briefing"* begins, that Bartlett projects confidence and knowledge. He focuses on the project's core activity and immediately catches the committee's attention by starting with *"the first tunnel."* From his dialogue, you can see he has a fundamental grasp of the problems *(tunnel length)* and the associated risks *(detection)*. He stuns his project team by the audacity of the plan and the details of where the tunnels are going to be located. We'll explore this more in the next section. For now, let's continue.

Willie: All right, Roger. But did you say **"the first tunnel"**?

Bartlett: I did. There will be three. We'll call them Tom, Dick, and Harry. Tom, as I said, goes out directly east from 104. Dick goes north from the kitchen, and Harry goes out parallel to Tom from 105. If the goons find one, we'll move into the other.

MacDonald: How many men do you plan to take out, Roger?

Bartlett: Two hundred and fifty.

[Shocked stares]

Bartlett: There will be no half-measures this time, gentlemen. There will be identification papers and documents for everyone. And Griff, we'll need outfits for the lot.

Griffith: Two hundred and fifty?

Bartlett: Mostly civilian clothes.

Griffith: Yes, but, um... okay, Roger.

Bartlett: Mac. Maps, blankets, rations, compasses for all the walkers, and timetables for every train.

MacDonald: Right, Roger.

   [Colin Blythe, known as **"the forger,"** enters]

Colin: Sorry I'm late, Roger.

Bartlett: It's all right, Colin. Sit down. We're going to tunnel.

Colin: Splendid.

Bartlett: Willie, you and Danny will be tunnel kings. Danny, you'll be in charge of traps, and I'll work out the exact location with you tomorrow.

Danny: Good.

Bartlett: Sedgwick, manufacturer. Griffith, as I said, tailor. Nimmo and Hayes, diversions. Mac, of course, will take care of intelligence. Hendley? We haven't met. Scrounger? Right. Dennis, maps and surveys. Colin, you'll take your usual job. Eric, how are you gonna get rid of this dirt?

Eric: Usual places. I hadn't anticipated three tunnels, but we'll manage.

It is clear that Barlett has an astounding grasp of the details and team roles and strengths and has thought of all the risks in advance. The next question regards security.

Sorren: Roger, who's going to handle security for all this?

Bartlett: You are. I want a system of stooges covering this compound from front to back, checking every goon in and out. I want a signal system so perfect that if ever a ferret gets within 50 feet of any of the huts in which we're working, we can shut down without a sign. Well, I don't think there's much point in discussing any more now. I'll meet each of you on the exercise circuit, we'll pound out the details. Nothing else, is there, Mac?

MacDonald: I shouldn't think so, Roger.

🎬 "ACTION!!!" PROJECTLAND SUCCESS TIPS

One of the things I love about this movie is that there are so many helpful lessons for us about how to operate in the stressful pressure cooker of Projectland. In fact, projects can be under pressure from day one: scrutinized, questioned, and even targeted for early shutdown. To complete the project journey to implementation, projects need to be resilient with contingencies for every eventuality along the way. Hence the need for extensive planning using scenarios and risk management. This work starts with a well-planned and executed kickoff meeting.

Let's explore a few lessons and map what is happening in our movie moment to help us set our project people up for success.

KEEP KICKOFFS BRIEF AND FOCUSED

The Big X *(Bartlett)* is the Project Manager leading the escape project kickoff meeting. This has to be one of the shortest recorded kickoff meetings in the history of projects *(3 minutes 26 seconds)*.

Why was it so short? Because everyone understood the vision clearly, it didn't need to be any longer. It was well-prepared and clearly articulated.

He describes an outrageously bold vision incorporating a radical approach at a scale not considered before, especially challenging because of the limited resources available to the project team and the constraints of the inconducive environment. His vision is clever, because a three-tunnel plan decreases the risk of shutdown and increases options for the team. For instance, if one of the tunnels was threatened or under suspicion, work could be halted for that tunnel but continued on another one.

ENSURE THE TEAM FULLY UNDERSTANDS AND COMPREHENDS THE PROJECT

What does the kickoff scene say about Big X's understanding of the project? The questions and statements are packed with information. Each one suggests a substantial set of activities that lead to the project's major deliverables.

Big X is refusing no half-measures or compromises. In other words, he wants to throw everything at this plan to make it the greatest escape of all time. Nothing on that scale has ever been considered and requires a project scope of tremendous size and complexity. Such an increase over the normal scope of a prison escape, a scale of a factor of ten, requires new ways of thinking and fresh approaches and solutions.

Big X has an absolutely comprehensive grasp of the project scope—and in today's language from the Project Management Institute, the *Work Breakdown Structure (the hierarchical representation of the scope in terms of deliverables)*—not only in the minutia of digging the tunnels, but in the complexity of the project and its many constraints that must be overcome to give the escapers a reasonable chance of success.

KNOW YOUR TEAM

What does the delivery and its style say about the Big X? He exudes absolute confidence, and his plan is to ensure nothing gets in their way. Astutely, he paces through the group because he is part of it.

Big X understands how to organize the project into functional departments that create the major deliverables of the Work Breakdown Structure. He also knows his project team extremely well, their skill sets and the experience they have, and who is best suited to lead these departments.

Meanwhile, as each member of the Escape Committee is assigned their role and department, they accept full responsibility without argument and start planning how they are going to deliver.

GET YOUR TEAM EXCITED AND MOTIVATED TO TAKE THE PROJECT ON

What did the meeting achieve? It provided motivation, and the green light to move forward. With this level of clarity, everyone on the Escape Committee understood how they were going to fit in and the role they were going to take.

Big X expands on the complexity of the project where digging tunnels is only half of the project scope. Preparing the escapers is a monumental activity if they are to stand any chance of survival. Griffith's quick response to the request to have 250 outfits ready for the team highlights how there is a very quick buy-in to the plan even though the activities are monumental in scale.

The last question from Sorren regarding security highlights the hidden aspects of the project scope not immediately obvious to the viewer. But even to that, Big X has an answer; he's really thought through the solutions that need to be put in place to address escape prevention measures.

Overall Big X's description of the project is so comprehensive he can bring the meeting to a close with the minimum of questions or fuss.

A GREAT KICKOFF MEETING BEGINS TO CREATE A "CAN DO" SPIRIT FOR YOUR PROJECT TEAM, NO MATTER HOW TOXIC THE REST OF THE ORGANIZATION IS

What happens as a result of this meeting? In the rest of the movie, we discover how everything in Stalag Luft III was set up to prevent escape. The hostile environment was ripe for a project failure. The project planning and preparation were hindered everyday by new risks introduced by the captors, such as new escape prevention measures or changes in routine. The Escape Committee created an atmosphere where everything was thought possible. In my experience, some corporate environments are completely inconducive to projects and specifically by design, too!

AN INSPIRED AND MOTIVATED TEAM WILL WORK PROACTIVELY TO OVERCOME CHALLENGES

What did this positive *"can do"* culture lead to? It enabled them to more easily mitigate risks, and feel confident continuously testing, refining ideas, and finding solutions to the risks. The Escape Committee overcame continuous difficulties literally thrown at them, and ran the project in an agile way to keep it from shutting down within the budget and resources available to them.

Great kickoff meetings require meticulous preparation so they can be succinct, to the point, and flow naturally.

📢 DIRECTOR'S COMMENTS

It was not immediately obvious to me that the *escape* was a project, and excellent project management made it *great*.

Many projects today are initiated with clear objectives, executive sponsorship, and a healthy budget, but still fail. Other projects have no budgets, many obstacles in their way, and succeed. This movie is largely viewed as a success story and a wonderful case study for this latter scenario.

As I studied the movie further, I realized that the clandestine kick-off meeting scene draws the audience into a secret project and the planning process, heightening the expectations and tensions of what could possibly happen during the remainder of the movie.

The scene is riveting because of the sense of brilliant leadership and teamwork. Not much has to be said in the kickoff meeting, as the communication is so clear that the team inherently understands what must be done, by whom, and when, based on planning informed by previous experience and project failures.

I find the language between the characters intriguing. As a viewer, I want to know what a scrounger is and does; what are goons, ferrets and traps; and why the tunnels are named Tom, Dick, and Harry *(they are code words meant to ensure nobody would blurt out the word tunnel)*.

The scene also lays down the gauntlet of what to expect. It sets up the viewer to want to see the solutions come to life for how the project team will overcome all the escape prevention measures.

I found this movie to be so ripe with lessons, that I wrote an entire book on it, *Project Lessons from the Great Escape*.

🎬 REALITY SHOW: WHEN LIFE IMITATES ART

This one scene has stuck with me through my career and every time I start a new project with a kickoff meeting, I run through what Big X did in terms of his preparation and delivery. In my experience this is the most important meeting of the project. Done well, it sets the tone for the entire project. Done poorly, it requires extensive recovery. If the meeting is going to run for one hour, then I spend 40 hours preparing for it. In the few projects that I didn't get this preparation time because I was given the project late in the day, the effectiveness of the kickoffs suffered and I struggled for the next couple of months to get the project back on track.

🎬 "IT'S A WRAP!"

The next time you are planning a project kickoff meeting, prepare! You need to clearly understand why the project is being undertaken. If a *"benefit analysis"* exists, this can help you understand the organization's rationale for approving the project *(the why)*. Next, you need to have a comprehensive grasp of the project scope *(the what)* and all the constraints of the environment that will need to be navigated *(the how)*. From this foundation *(the why, what, and how)*, you and your team can begin to identify the project risks, estimate the true project cost, and create a realistic project schedule. Then, you can develop a believable Cost vs. Benefit Analysis and Business Case. When you have all of this it can help align executive leadership's expectations and the team responsible for delivering. Only then will confidence be sky high, because the project can move forward on the right footing with everyone marching in lockstep together and ready to overcome the odds.

🎬 PRESENTED BY...

MARK KOZAK-HOLLAND PHD, PMP, IPMA-D, CERT.APM, CMP

Mark Kozak-Holland is a Senior Project Manager/Consultant, author, and trainer. His 40+year professional career interweaves consulting, research, and writing.

With major project-based services organizations, such as Tandem Computers, IBM and HP/HPe, and as part of strategic consulting teams, he has delivered over 200 client-facing professional service engagements, initiating and managing complex programs/projects, transformations, and organizational change.

As research consultant, in 1994 he founded *Lessons-from-History (LFH)*, a unique consultancy that helps organizations reach a sustainable future by offering ideas, practices, and solutions from the past to help others avoid repeating mistakes and to capture time-proven techniques. LFH is an innovative means of assisting organizations and their leaders to survive and succeed in today's demanding marketplace.

Mark's research and experience shows that societies move through repeating cycles of disruptive change triggered by enabling technologies. He created the LFH publication series which reinterprets our past and explains the impact of innovation, enabling technologies, projects, and transformation for today's business world. LFH takes periods of great transition like the Industrial Revolution and identifies relevant historical case studies. It reinterprets these through different business lenses, such as project management, management, and operations management, and extracts knowledge, best practices, and lessons learned.

He augmented this approach with academic research completed for his Ph.D. in the disciplines of business and project management. He established a methodology for identifying, synthesizing and interpreting lessons from case studies and transformational projects from the past for today. He has a set of academic publications which he draws on in all his work including advanced project management training for senior professionals.

Project Lessons from the Great Escape was Dr. Kozak-Holland's third book in the LFH series, and the kickoff scene is one of his favorites highlighted therein.

Mark resides in Ontario, Canada from where he widely travels in his pursuit of uncovering lessons from history for today's world.

CHAPTER 4

DO YOU KNOW WHAT YOU'RE DOING?

Trusting Your Approach, But Planning for Detours *(Ocean's 11)*

Ocean's Eleven
Logline: "Danny Ocean, a gangster, rounds up a gang of associates to stage a sophisticated and elaborate casino heist which involves robbing three Las Vegas casinos simultaneously during a popular boxing event."[4]

SETTING THE SCENE

DANNY OCEAN *(PLAYED BY GEORGE CLOONEY)* **IS A THIEF FRESH** out of jail and sets his sights on an ambitious, near-impossible project: robbing the casino owned by Terry Benedict *(Andy Garcia)*, the new fiancé of his ex-wife, Tess *(Julia Roberts)* on fight night. Meeting her in a restaurant, the following conversation ensues:

```
Tess: "Do you remember what I said to you when we
first met?"

Danny: "You said I'd better know what I'm doing."

Tess: "And do you? Because you should walk out that
door if you don't."

Danny: "I know what I'm doing."
```

This specific scene is primarily regarding their marriage, but the same theme rings throughout the movie.

HOT TAKE: Whether a project starts on the right foot or not, the only way you come out on the other side with your integrity intact is by doing it right, the first—or second—time around. In essence, know the destination, but trust your approach and prepare for detours.

THE MOVIE MOMENT

In an early scene, *doing it right the first time* is discussed. Danny Ocean seeks advice from Rusty Ryan *(Brad Pitt)* about the near-impossible gig he wants to undertake. Rusty says, ***"It's tricky. It's never been done before. You'll need planning, a large crew."*** Rusty goes on to make other suggestions and then they discuss finding a backer and the necessary team members.

Danny Ocean is the Project Manager, and Rusty is a Subject Matter Expert *(SME)*, helping to identify the critical roles and approach required to successfully complete the project.

In another scene, where the first task on the night of the heist is to trigger a power outage, there is an unexpected issue.

Basher Tarr *(Don Cheadle)*, informs the team that they've run into a major setback—to pull off the heist, they require a *pinch*, a device capable of creating a blackout through an electromagnetic pulse. Among the possible sources, Caltech, a research institution in the city, has one and they'll have to steal it.

"ACTION!!!" PROJECTLAND SUCCESS TIPS

Since projects are unique by definition, project managers can have projects on their hands they have never done before. And since projects by definition are temporary, that means there is a beginning, an end, and the clock is ticking. This translates into a sense of urgency, particularly when the team must hit a time target, like in the movie. Some projects also require spontaneous adaptation, especially when navigating around unexpected obstacles.

In these situations, imagine being asked: ***"Do you know what you're doing?"***

In the movie, this question came up at least three times in different ways: The first time when Danny's ex-wife, Tess, asked him at dinner. A second time when the sponsor, Reuben Tishkoff *(Elliott Gould)*, asked him if he was nuts, when he disclosed the plan. And a third time when team member, Saul Bloom *(Carl Reiner)*, asked questions concerning the risks, when the following dialogue ensued:

```
Saul: I have a question, say we get into the cage,
and through the security doors there and down the
elevator we can't move, and past the guards with the
guns, and into the vault we can't open...

Rusty: Without being seen by the cameras.

Danny: Oh yeah, sorry, I forgot to mention that.

Saul: Yeah well, say we do all that... uh... we're
just supposed to walk out of there with $150,000,000
in cash on us, without getting stopped?
```

A heist on this vault, which feeds three casinos, had *never been done before*. And this was a fixed-time project. It had to be done on fight night, when the vault would be overflowing with cash.

Danny was clear on the outcome desired, but not on how it was going to work out without landing himself back in jail along with everyone else. So he did the right things, just like a pro project manager would. He recruited an experienced, technical lead he trusted who knew what other competencies were required on the team. They met in person with the sponsor, who had the right motivation and financial means to support them. In other words, Danny put together what he felt was a foolproof plan and an expert team to deliver it.

Except in project management, nothing is foolproof.

While there was a plan, a few things changed while the project was in flight. For instance, others had to take more prominent roles when it became clear that Danny was emotionally vested, since Tess's fiancé was the owner of the casinos. The plan was also adjusted by the new scope that was required; stealing the pinch from Caltech, a key element required for the heist to succeed.

As they proceeded, the team was thrown several more obstacles they had to cleverly conquer. But what would have happened if Danny had been too prideful or overconfident and had started with the wrong tech lead, a team without the right skills, or a wishy-washy sponsor? What if the pinch heist wasn't successful and a complete plan overhaul was required?

Imagine starting wrongly. Does this imply the project ends wrongly? Or can you make adjustments once you realize your mistakes? Or imagine starting the right way. Does this ensure success? Not necessarily if unexpected obstacles appear and you don't have the savvy or a solid approach to make proper adjustments. Whether at the beginning or midway, what is the right way to operate to be able to confidently answer the question: *"Do you know what you're doing?"*

THE "RIGHT" WAY

There are reasons for methodologies, and there are very good reasons to confirm if an enterprise has one it actually follows. There are many project leaders who will lobby to avoid the enterprise's policies or standards. If there is truly an exception, someone should sign off on that exclusion.

While an exhaustive account about applying methodologies is beyond the scope of this chapter, the following are crucial on any project.

CLARIFY OBJECTIVES: KNOW THE END GOAL

In project management, a clear objective sets the stage for success. For Sponsor Reuben, Project Manager Danny, Trusted Tech Lead Rusty, and their skilled crew, the mission was to secure $150 million from the casinos, motivated by Danny's personal revenge and incredible financial gain for the team. This is akin to defining the business case or project proposal.

IDENTIFY KEY PLAYERS AND THEIR NEEDS

The heist's team members each had unique motivations. Danny and Rusty tailored the plan to address these needs, particularly Reuben's desire to see Terry humiliated *(which happened to align nicely with Danny's feelings)*. This is akin to ensuring that the vision is clear, and that there is one extrinsic motivation *(i.e., call to action)* for team members to commit to in pursuit of the successful completion of the project.

ENGAGE THE TEAM EARLY

ENGAGING THE TEAM EARLY HELPED UNCOVER KEY RISKS AND ensured they were on board. For instance, Reuben's financial backing came with the expectation of success, as it does for most project sponsors. This added pressure to address all risks effectively. And to make sure all the risks were addressed, the scene where Saul Bloom *(Carl Reiner)* deftly recapped the seemingly impossible plan during the briefing was necessary to ensure the team's concerns were articulated, discussed, and planned for. Team members do their best work when they feel confident in leadership and that the plan is feasible.

PLAN FOR RISKS

Danny and Rusty anticipated potential obstacles, such as Benedict's advanced security, tight timing for the operation, and the logistics of moving $150 million in cash. Risk response plans included employing Tess *(Danny's ex-wife and Terry's fiancé)* as leverage.

STAY FLEXIBLE: ROLLING WAVE PLANNING

Like real-world projects, the heist's planning evolved as new information emerged. For instance, discovering the need for a device that needed to be stolen mid-planning required adapting their strategy. Danny and Rusty planned immediate steps in detail while still leaving room to address future uncertainties.

THE PROJECT RECOVERY ALTERNATIVE

Sometimes, projects are faced with a need to re-prioritize, accommodate scope creep, or re-baseline. Of course, if you fail to start the right way to begin with, as outlined above, you increase the chances of this happening.

In any case, if you need to recover a project in trouble, or you're faced with *"we need a new plan,"* what should you do? Here are five suggested actions and their corresponding movie moments:

- **Assess the current situation:** Identify the root cause—e.g., scope creep, misalignment, unexpected risks, or lack of resources. When Danny Ocean *(George Clooney)* and the team discover the backup power source that could jeopardize their entire heist, they stop to analyze the implications—realizing it could compromise their core plan.
- **Engage key stakeholders:** Align with the sponsor, team leads, and impacted stakeholders to redefine priorities. In the movie, the team regroups to brainstorm a new plan—and Linus Caldwell *(Matt Damon)*, previously sidelined, is now given a key role. They also debate how to acquire the *pinch (an electromagnetic pulse device)*.
- **Re-baseline realistically:** Adjust timelines, resources, and deliverables while ensuring alignment with the original business objective. Frank Catton *(Bernie Mac)*, Basher Tarr *(Don Cheadle)*,

and Livingston Dell *(Eddie Jemison)* all recalibrate their roles to match the updated execution timeline. They run a new simulation using a replica vault to rework their entry and timing, recalibrating the entire operation to fit the updated scenario.
- **Communicate transparently:** Keep stakeholders informed of the changes, potential risks, and expected benefits. Helping the team understand the gravity of the situation at the onset was done well by Basher Tarr, prompting urgency and clarity on what's at stake. On the flip side, Danny Ocean was compelled to come out to the group regarding his interests in the heist outside money, and that was a risk they all needed to have been aware of at the beginning.
- **Focus on the end goal:** Even with setbacks, maintain focus on delivering the business benefits that justify the project. Despite the chaos, Danny Ocean keeps everyone focused on the outcome—pulling off the heist cleanly and ensuring each crew member walks away with their cut.

🎬 DIRECTOR'S COMMENTS

When Tess asked if Danny knew what he was doing, and he answered, *"I know what I'm doing,"* it did not imply he had everything figured out *(a good marriage or the scope of the heist)*. It only implied he knew how to do it right, trusted his ability to figure it out along the way, and was going to focus his attention on the process and try to set his emotions aside.

When a complex, risky project that's never been done before kicks off, start with an objective framework that has worked before, or an enterprise-approved methodology. If the project kicked off, went off track, and then you were brought in to salvage it, ask for an opportunity to *"do it right"* this second time around and re-baseline *(e.g., establish a new official "plan of record")*. Otherwise, like Tess told Danny, that would be your chance to walk away.

If you don't feel you can lead the project to a successful conclusion, it's best to say so. Your integrity is at stake. I have seen project managers scared to honestly assess the current state and present the data to gain approval for a new plan. Changes happen ALL the time and re-baselining shouldn't be perceived as a failure—it will be a badge of honor for a project manager who can navigate the storm, help the sponsor and team prioritize, and steer the ship of competent sailors to safe harbor. With a new plan re-started the right way—even without having executed that type of project before—when you're asked the question: ***"Do you know what you're doing?"*** you will not second guess yourself.

🎬 REALITY SHOW: WHEN LIFE IMITATES ART

Of the many regulatory compliance projects I have been on, there was one where I was tasked with implementing new member notification letters through a corporate platform. On the surface, the goal was straightforward: create compliant letters and integrate them into both online and offline communications. But making this happen was anything but simple.

From the start, the project was a case study in misalignment. The organization was piloting Scrum *(i.e., Agile methodology-driven)* implementations, but hadn't informed the senior project managers involved. They didn't even know the project was part of the pilot until a Scrum Master was introduced. This person had to conduct role delineation sessions to clarify everyone's responsibilities before establishing a team working agreement *(i.e., an agreed-upon set of team guidelines)*.

At the same time, the Corporate Communications team was undergoing a brand revamp, but wasn't engaged early enough to approve designs, leading to delays. Additionally, during the initiation phase of the project, the enterprise solution architect had produced a ***"current vs. future state"*** Enterprise Data Flow diagram, giving business leaders the false hope that this would be a walk in the park.

Meanwhile, there was no engagement with the lines of business supporting the systems to understand if there were challenges the new system design wasn't going to solve. They needed a ***"Saul Bloom"*** on the project *(recalling Carl Reiner's exhaustive recounting of the possible challenges and risks)*.

At the cross-functional team level, the Data Solutions, Digital Transformation, and Client Communications teams were supposed to collaborate but had wildly different levels of engagement and priorities.

As it turns out, I was the Scrum Master brought in. And I asked myself the question, ***"Do you know what you're doing?"***

When it became clear the original plan was unsalvageable, I had to pivot fast. The only way forward was to create a new plan. But the original deadline was a fixed one and had to be met. The senior project manager and her backup were the next to ask me: ***"Do you know what you're doing?"***

I worked with the technology and solution leads and the approach went like this:

1. **Aligning Sponsors on New Releases:** I facilitated conversations with sponsors to identify a minimum viable product *(MVP)* for regulatory compliance. Originally, the team had planned for twenty-two letters, and we were able to agree on an MVP with only four. Whew! High-priority developments were redefined to meet the original hard deadline, while lower-priority items were shifted to post-project operations.

2. **Reprioritizing Tasks:** I worked with the teams to redefine deliverables, focusing on what was critical for compliance while shelving non-essential tasks.

3. **Engaging Reluctant Teams**: The Digital Transformation team, touted as the *"Agile mature experts,"* had been largely absent during solution design and development iterations *(called Sprints in Agile methodology)*. I had to leverage the influence of their leaders to help them understand the project's urgency and its impact on the enterprise, and ensure they delivered their part.

4. **Streamlining Deployment:** Already missed production deployment schedules threatened to derail the project further. We introduced a workback schedule, reverse-engineering the timelines in close partnership with the Enterprise Release Management engineering team, who owned the performance test and production environments, as well as the schedule that allowed us to go live.

🎬 "IT'S A WRAP!"

When trusted with bringing an initiative to life or helping a business meet specific objectives, doing it right, whether at the beginning, or midway, is almost ALWAYS possible. Curveballs happen, but when asked: *"Do you know what you're doing?"* it's not a solution question, it's an *"approach"* question and you shouldn't second-guess yourself.

🎬 PRESENTED BY...

JUSTUS AIYELA

Justus Aiyela is a dynamic Senior PMO Lead and Program Manager recognized for driving strategic alignment, agile delivery, and operational excellence across complex, high-stakes programs. With globally respected certifications—including PMP, LSSBB, SAFe 6 Agilist, and CSP-SM—he currently leads a $100M+ project portfolio within a Shared Services PMO, managing over 30 initiatives while ensuring regulatory compliance and financial stewardship.

A trusted mentor and educator, Justus has trained more than 500 professionals, including senior military leaders, in project management and Lean Six Sigma. He holds a Master's in Data Management & Analytics and brings a sharp focus on innovation, transformation, and empowering teams for impact.

Beyond his day commitments, Justus is the host of *Life & IT Project Management* YouTube channel, where he collaborates with elite professionals to share actionable insights and elevate the next generation of project leaders.

Justus lives in Canada, and enjoys spending time with his wife and son.

CHAPTER 5

"I'VE NEVER DONE IT, BUT I'VE ALWAYS DREAMED OF IT!"

Lessons in Attitude from an Unlucky Italian Accountant *(Fantozzi)*

Fantozzi (AKA White Collar Blues)
Logline: "A good-natured but unlucky Italian is constantly getting into difficult situations, but never loses his positive mood."[5]

SETTING THE SCENE

HOW MANY TIMES DID YOU FIND YOURSELF IN A SITUATION where things did not go as planned? Being stuck at a crossroad, tangled with other cars and with all traffic lights out of order? Dressing up for an appointment, and discovering your favorite dress is dirty, or the zip is broken, or the appointment is cancelled? Cooking dinner and realizing you don't have that necessary ingredient you were sure was in the cupboard? Packing your car for your vacation, and when it's all done with the trunk full and you're ready to go, you realize that a tire is flat?

We've all been there.

And if you've ever been involved in a project, you surely have observed that projects rarely go accordingly to plan. The truth is that no matter how good your plan is or how low your risks are, you will frequently find yourself in unexpected situations.

What to do then? How to react? You could start complaining about it. Or stay there, stuck, immobilized by the events. Or you can acknowledge the situation, roll up your sleeves, and tackle the challenges that Projectland throws at you.

Adapting to the changing conditions, being flexible, looking for creative solutions, staying positive despite the difficulties, are all parts of an attitude you must have if you want to be successful in your projects, and on a wider perspective, in your life.

That's exactly what happens in *Fantozzi*. The main character, Ugo Fantozzi, is a kind-hearted, friendly, and terribly unlucky accountant who represents the average Italian office worker of a big corporation of the 1970s. He is in a constant battle against absurd challenges he encounters in everything he does. Whether he is playing a football match with colleagues, celebrating New Year's Eve, having a camping vacation with his friend, or simply going to the office in the morning, life always has something unexpected in store for him.

No matter how chaotic or absurd the circumstances, he persists—embodying resilience, creativity, and an indomitable spirit. Fantozzi's attitude is a lesson in perseverance and adaptability, qualities that resonate deeply with those of us who live in Projectland!

This is perfectly represented in the iconic sketch **"Going to work"**, a journey that transforms a mundane commute into a heroic quest.

> **HOT TAKE:** Having a plan helps, but when reality hits you in the face—and it often does—being creative, adaptable, persistent, and positive makes all the difference between failure and success.

🍿 THE MOVIE MOMENT

After a brief opening-credits montage to introduce the unlucky accountant Fantozzi, the **"Going to work"** segment begins. As Fantozzi's alarm clock goes off, narration reveals:

In order to stamp his punch card and clock in exactly at 8:30, Fantozzi used to wake up at 06:15. That was 16 years ago. Today, after many experiments and improvements, he wakes up at 7:51... pushing the limit of human capabilities.

The scene unfolds, illustrating that everything is calculated to the second: 5 seconds to regain consciousness; 4 seconds to overcome the daily impact of seeing his frumpy wife, and 6 more seconds to ask himself—as always with no plausible answer—what made him marry that kind of **"domestic creature."** It takes 3 seconds to drink Mrs. Pina's *(Fantozzi's wife's)* abominable espresso *(at 3,000°F!)*. From 8 to 10 seconds to cool down his burned tongue at the bathroom sink. 2.5 seconds to kiss his daughter Mariangela, followed by drinking a café latte while simultaneously brushing his hair, then brushing his teeth with a disgusting mix of menthol and coffee flavor. This all results in **"instantaneous pressing physiological needs"** that he can complete in the European record time of just 6 seconds.

This leaves him with a fortune of three minutes to get dressed *(with his wife's help)* and run to the bus stop to catch the 08:01 bus. Of course, this tight schedule is possible only without unforeseen accidents happening.

And in this exact moment, the lace of his right shoe breaks. Fantozzi's wife, Pina, dives into a drawer to rummage for a new lace. She finds one of a different color, ties it to the broken one and wraps the shoe with tape, just to make it work. And so he continues.

However, he now realizes the time wasted by the lace mishap has set him back irrevocably; he had been unable to follow the pre-established plan. This is when Fantozzi has a brilliant and unexpected idea: to catch the bus on the fly by jumping from the balcony and thus saving two minutes!

His wife and daughter try to stop him, pointing out that he does not have the right physique and that jumping from the balcony to catch the bus on the fly is something he has never done before.

"I've never done it, but I've always dreamed of it!," says Fantozzi, proudly.

With these words, the never-say-die Fantozzi jumps from the balcony, runs across the street, and with the encouraging voices of the neighbors leaning out of their balconies, he manages, albeit with great difficulty, to catch the bus on the fly as it races past. However, as he has jumped onto the back of another passenger who was hanging out of the open bus doors, he causes a chain reaction—with every passenger falling out of the bus one-by-one onto the street.

The problems of Fantozzi's morning do not end here, however. After a few other dramas exaggerated with comic hyperbole, Fantozzi, in an ambulance, manages to arrive at the entrance of the *"Megaditta,"* the massive corporation for which he works. Finally, after a last-gasp race, he succeeds in his epic quest to punch his badge at 8:30 sharp.

"ACTION!!!" PROJECTLAND SUCCESS TIPS

Fantozzi is a comedy, surreal, yet profound in that it includes many life lessons and offers plenty of food for thought. Looking at it through the eyes of a project manager, there are some elements that particularly resonate with those who professionally navigate Projectland.

The first that absolutely must be considered is the importance of **planning**. Not the importance of the plan itself, the artifact, but the importance of the act of planning. My favorite quote on this subject is one attributed to the former American president Dwight D. Eisenhower: *"In preparing for battle I have always found that plans are useless, but planning is indispensable."*

In the *"Going to work"* scene, Fantozzi planned every activity down to the last second, from setting the alarm clock to punching the badge—and we know how that ended. In other parts of the movie, as in all the subsequent Fantozzi films, the key figure of the *planner* is his colleague and friend, the accountant Filini. Filini organizes and plans everything: soccer games among colleagues, trips out of town, company parties, and so on. It is Filini who initiates almost all the tragic initiatives that Fantozzi, unfortunately feels forced to participate in.

So, if plans never go *"accordingly to the plan,"* why is planning so important? Planning, in its essence, is not about creating a perfect roadmap that avoids all obstacles, but about understanding your goals, evaluating possible scenarios, examining the associated risks, and preparing to manage uncertainty. Fantozzi shows that even when plans inevitably fail, the act of planning allows you to think quickly, adapt to the situation and solve problems creatively.

These are two other key elements in Projectland: *flexibility* and the *ability to adapt*. It's important to be aware that there are many ways to achieve the result. It is beneficial to be proactive in looking for the best path, even if it deviates from the initial plan. It's also helpful to remain flexible and to be able to react quickly when things don't go as expected. For example, Fantozzi had to expeditiously find a solution for the broken string, and then implement his brilliant balcony back-up plan to recover lost time and achieve his goal.

When it comes to *creativity* in solving problems, unfortunately it is an approach that is not often found in Projectland, but something I believe can be a great added value. Too often when the predefined planned path does not work, the team looks for a solution as close as possible to the initial one. What if instead we approached the problem differently? Asking better questions and looking at challenges and solutions from a different perspective is a way to improve your out-of-the-box thinking and potentially find more creative ways to achieve your goals.

We've learned that planning is essential, preparing for the challenges ahead is important, and remaining flexible and adaptable is crucial.

However, these elements alone are not enough without determination, a positive attitude, and an absolute belief that you can achieve what you want. These aspects contribute to forming the right attitude, the right mindset you need to have in Projectland. Analyzing Fantozzi, you clearly see that his *attitude is everything*. More than a *"can-do"* attitude, it is a *"will-do"* attitude. Despite the absurd challenges thrown his way, he will achieve what he needs to do: punching his badge at 8:30 sharp.

📢 DIRECTOR'S COMMENTS

I think you would not find many Italians who grew up in Italy during the '70s, '80s, or '90s who are not deeply connected with *Fantozzi*. Most are—I am definitely one of them. We recognize ourselves in Fantozzi and his world. The routine of the average day-to-day life, the relationship with his wife and daughter, the difficulties with the neighbors, the interactions with the colleagues, the disrespectful behaviors of management and people with power, the bureaucracy of the system, and the misfortune of the average working-class person.

Fantozzi is one of the rare movies of the last 50 years that have impacted and changed the Italian culture and language. Many terms and behaviors have officially entered the Italian dictionaries and become part of Italian life.

As an Italian living abroad, I have the opportunity to appreciate the genius of Fantozzi even more. The strong contrast between the flexibility, the adaptability, the art of finding creative solutions to any type of problem, which are very common in Italy; is strongly opposed to what I've found in some other countries where everything is predetermined and must follow strict rules and a rigorous plan. And when the plan does not work? Their typical response is to repeat the steps, and continue to try following the initial plan, because *"so it is written."* A drastically different approach than Fantozzi.

I can personally relate to the sketch, *"Going to work."* When I was around 14 years old and I started going to high school, I was forced to change my morning routine. The school was in a central location in Milan (*we call it Milano*), while I was living with my parents in the suburbs. The change of location, compared to my previous school, required me to wake up earlier, manage different dependencies with my parents' schedules, and take a couple of buses. Add to this journey the additional time required to prepare when you evolve from a kid into a teenager, and you have the perfect recipe for a morning disaster.

Like Fantozzi, I started by setting my alarm clock incredibly early. With the passing of the days and the lessons learned, I pushed it, and pushed it, until it almost reached *"the limit of human capabilities."* When I started arriving all-too-frequently late at school, I re-worked my morning routine, but without success. Trying to optimize something that had serious design flaws was not getting me anywhere. After a few weeks, I could no longer stand the rushing and the anxiety of having not enough time to prepare, having too many risks, and having to catch the bus on the fly.

One day, I decided to take a different approach. I realized it was not so bad to wake up a bit earlier and plan activities in a way that would not clash with the other family members. Since that day, I am the one waking up early, taking time for my morning routine, and using that well-managed time as a preparation phase for a successful day.

REALITY SHOW: WHEN LIFE IMITATES ART

A good high-level plan beats a perfect one. During my years in Projectland, I have managed many projects where the plan became obsolete quite soon after it was *"done."* One project in particular brings back a special memory. I was a rather young project manager, and this was my first big project. We were at the beginning of the project, and together with my project team and my project planner, we worked diligently to create an initial detailed plan. There were hundreds of lines in that plan, every task was scheduled to the very last detail. Previously, in every other project I managed before this one, I never had such a long and detailed plan. We thought we were doing great work by having such a detailed plan. We had thought of everything.

Two weeks after the big plan was published, my planner informed me that we had a problem. A team member charged time on a task that was scheduled to take place almost at the end of the project. Without going into details, with the tool we used back then and its limitations, this mistake created a series of issues with the task dependencies and made the plan unusable. To fix the issue, my planner and I spent hours adjusting the plan. I also had a conversation with that team member to ensure he understood the mistake, so that he could avoid it in future. The mistake he made was assuming the key user training would qualify as user acceptance testing. I believe he was looking for a shortcut by skipping user acceptance testing altogether.

Right after I thought we had resolved this painful issue, the following week, another team member made the same mistake! And for the very same reason as the first guy. Just like the first time, we followed the same pattern. We spent hours making the tedious necessary adjustments to the plan, and I had to speak with this team member, too. The following week, we were in the same situation again. This was when I concluded that it's useless to spend *(waste?)* time on adjusting such a long, detailed plan that can easily be misunderstood or glossed over *(it's hard to see the forest for the trees)*. I decided to go back to my usual approach of a simple high-level plan, which guarantees direction, is easy to maintain, and is clear enough for everyone.

I never had that issue again; not in that project, nor in future projects. The extra benefit was that I finally could spend time on actually leading the project and not on designing the perfect plan. Having a perfect plan is impossible and misses the point entirely. The point is ensuring the team is aligned on the project objectives, the activities to perform, the possible options, and is prepared to manage uncertainty.

Important decisions are often difficult (and don't have to come from the top). One afternoon, we made the decision to pause our pilot project and move ahead with another project. At the time, I did not realize how important that decision was. I was leading a big program, the biggest in the organization, and we had strong sponsorship from the executive who wanted to transform the way our company was organized. We were conducting the process/tool discovery phase for the location identified as the pilot project in that program. The work between the global team and the local onsite team was intense, but progressing smoothly.

Suddenly, two days before the conclusion of the discovery phase, the onsite management team changed their minds: a 180-degree shift. Despite having been formerly on board and eager to implement the process changes, they were suddenly completely against them and concocted their own highly inaccurate business case to oppose the initiative. We spent days trying to understand what had happened and identify scope adjustments that could potentially allow our program to proceed. We had many conversations with our stakeholders, but there was no way to find common ground. The easiest way forward, which was also the one our executive sponsor wanted, was to push the solution anyway and continue with that pilot project. Maybe an easy decision but surely the wrong one.

This was when we proposed our version of *"taking the bus on the fly."* We proposed to pause the activities in that pilot project and to move to another manufacturing site, the next feasible one on our program roadmap. It might not seem so dramatic, but it was absolutely a difficult decision for a traditional, structured organization. It was a proposal coming from the bottom, the program team, and not from the top. Also, it was complex to implement. We had to mobilize a whole new team and plan activities for another location of 1,000+ employees who weren't expecting any such changes until the following year. It wasn't easy, but our proposal was accepted, and the program progressed well. The new project was a huge success for the organization and showed other manufacturing sites that the outcome was well worth the effort.

Inspire, don't motivate. I had the pleasure to lead many PMOs in my career, and every team, every individual, has their special place close to my heart. One PMO was at a very low maturity level when I joined to lead their transformation into an efficient *Strategy Realization Office*—a transformation we never fully achieved, but that's another story. When I joined that team, I wasn't surprised by their low maturity and their low project management knowledge, but I was especially taken aback by their lack of motivation and their lack of belief in a better future. Me being me, I approached the situation as I did with previous teams. I spent time with them, I listened, and I showed them my vision for the future. I communicated it clearly, and I ensured everyone understood it.

As expected, not everyone wanted to embark on that journey with me. And that's okay. Those who wanted to be part of it slowly started to transform their behavior and began to enjoy the journey. Day after day, it was increasingly visible how they were beginning to approach things differently, how they finally learned to collaborate, and how they started spending time on improving their skills. Their renewed motivation was clear for all to see.

A few weeks passed by, and I had a face-to-face meeting with our human resources director. She was impressed by the transformation she saw in the members of my team. Delighted, I smiled. She smiled back and she added, *"Everyone can see it, Bruno. You're really good at motivating people."* To which I replied, *"I do not motivate people. I inspire them, and thanks to that inspiration they find the motivation within themselves."* Attitude is everything, and this is the right attitude to have in Projectland, and especially as the leader of any team. Be a model of optimism and determination. Show your team that a better future is possible, show them how to get there, make them feel they are going somewhere good, and inspire them to continue to move forward.

🎬 "IT'S A WRAP!"

Here are the three takeaways that I am sure will help you on your journey through Projectland.

If plan A doesn't work, there are many more letters in the alphabet. As soon as a plan is complete, it is already obsolete. However, the effort invested in planning builds the understanding of the project's goals, the possible paths to follow, and the associated risks. It prepares your project team to adapt dynamically, just as Fantozzi does when his morning commute turns into an obstacle course. Planning is an investment in your project's future. It prepares you for improvisation, and in Projectland, that's often what makes the difference between failure and success. While planning provides direction, flexibility ensures that progress continues even when the road takes an unexpected turn. Being flexible doesn't mean abandoning structure, but it does mean maintaining your focus on the goal while staying open to alternative paths to get there.

Change is the only constant. In Projectland, as in life, change is inevitable. And with the speed of change we are experiencing today, being ready for change is not enough. We need to embrace change. Proactively looking for opportunities to improve, learning new things, finding new ways to solve problems, are the best ways to improve our ability to adapt to changing conditions. We must be part of the change. Project success often depends on how well and how fast the project team adapts to shifting priorities, and how we face unexpected challenges. Do not limit yourself to simple minor adjustments of the initial plan. Dare to think differently, question assumptions, and experiment. Sometimes, the best solutions are reachable only by thinking outside the box, like Fantozzi did, by catching the bus on the fly.

Attitude is everything. One of the key characteristics of Fantozzi is his optimism. Even in the most absurd and challenging situations, whether undergoing his boss's unreasonable demands or dealing with personal misfortunes, he never loses his belief that things can improve and a better future is possible. His attitude and his determination help him push through when others might give up. A positive attitude is the foundation of success in projects, no matter your role—and quite possibly in life too. In Projectland, leaders who model positivity and determination, inspire their teams to stay motivated and face challenges head-on. Even when the situation seems to be *"at the limit of human capabilities,"* as Fantozzi would say, the right attitude will help you to find solutions and drive your project forward to a successful outcome.

🎬 PRESENTED BY...

BRUNO MORGANTE

Bruno is an outcome-driven leader who *solves problems and delivers results*. Yes, this is how he introduces himself.

With over 20 years of experience leading PMOs in large multinational organizations, he has consistently enabled businesses to achieve their strategic goals by building high-performing teams, improving processes, and managing extensive portfolios of concurrent projects.

Until the end of 2024, he served as the Global Head of PMO for a Fortune 500 company. Now, through his own company, Mantegora, Bruno aims to fulfil his purpose of *"Making the world a better place by empowering people and delivering impact."*

Mantegora provides business and management consultancy services to organizations and individuals, specializing in project management, leadership, and transformation. They partner with clients to align initiatives with strategic objectives, improve project delivery, and develop effective PMOs and project management teams through tailored advice, training, and operational support.

In his coaching and mentoring work, Bruno empowers individuals on their development journeys, offering guidance on leadership, personal growth, career development, and project management.

As a speaker, Bruno captivates audiences with dynamic keynotes filled with inspiring stories that motivate and drive action.

Bruno was born and raised in Milano, Italy, lives in Berlin, Germany, and is deeply in love with his wife's hometown, Krakow, Poland, as well as his wife.

Learn more about Bruno at brunomorgante.com and mantegora.com.

CHAPTER 6

"I HAVE A BAD FEELING ABOUT THIS"

Risk Management Insights from the Galactic Empire *(Star Wars)*

STAR WARS: Episode V – The Empire Strikes Back
Logline: "After the Empire overpowers the Rebel Alliance, Luke Skywalker begins training with Jedi Master Yoda, while Darth Vader and bounty hunter Boba Fett pursue his friends across the galaxy."[6]

SETTING THE SCENE

HAN SOLO *(PLAYED BY HARRISON FORD)* IS AN ADVENTUROUS smuggler, reluctant hero, and captain of the Millenium Falcon, the fastest old starship in the galaxy. He's well known by moviegoers for, among other things, two memorable quotes: ***"Never Tell Me the Odds"*** and ***"I have a bad feeling about this."*** The latter has become a hallmark of the Star Wars saga, spoken countless times by multiple characters—and even parodied outside the films. Knowing when to be bold and when to be cautious is more an art than a science, depending on confidence, risk tolerance, awareness, and many other factors.

Sometimes, an adventurer like Han Solo may border on the foolish side of boldness, but in a story where heroes overcome incredible odds, it works. On the other hand, Han has great confidence in his abilities—as any pilot would need—and even he knows when to keep his wits about him in dangerous territory.

HOT TAKE: When managing risk on projects, the key is balancing the overly optimistic "Never tell me the odds" and the decidedly pessimistic "I have a bad feeling about this."

THE MOVIE MOMENT

In *Star Wars: Episode V – The Empire Strikes Back (1980)*, during a daring escape from the evil empire, Han Solo pilots the Millennium Falcon and heads straight into an asteroid field to shake off enemy fighters. Ever the worrier, his companion, the protocol droid C-3PO, warns him, ***"Sir, the possibility of successfully navigating an asteroid field is approximately 3,720 to one!"*** Han's brash reply: ***"Never tell me the odds."*** *(Spoiler alert: He makes it out unscathed—because, well, he's Han Solo, and it's the movies.)*

Another famous line captures the feeling of impending risk: ***"I have a bad feeling about this."*** Luke Skywalker first utters it in *Star Wars: Episode IV – A New Hope* as the Millennium Falcon approaches the ominous Death Star. Han echoes the sentiment later when trapped in a trash compactor. Throughout the saga, variations of the phrase signal moments when characters face danger, uncertainty, or hesitation—reminding us that caution and unease naturally arise when navigating risk.

Time and again, Star Wars heroes wrestle with choices ranging from reckless boldness to careful planning. Obi-Wan Kenobi sums up this tension when he asks Luke, ***"Who is more foolish: the fool, or the fool who follows him?"*** The Force itself, the mystical energy binding the galaxy, symbolizes balance—the lesson being that wise decision-making requires weighing daring action against prudence.

"ACTION!!!" PROJECTLAND SUCCESS TIPS

Han Solo's optimistic ***"Never tell me the odds"*** and the foreboding ***"I have a bad feeling about this"*** are the perfect allegories for risk management in projects. As a project leader, you want to exude confidence, yet you bear responsibility for managing risks realistically. So, if your inner C-3PO leans over your shoulder to say, ***"Eh-hem, the odds of completing this project on time and within budget with inadequate resources are approximately 3,720 to one,"*** it's worth listening carefully.

On the other hand, if after thoughtful risk assessment you decide the rewards justify the risk, then it's full speed ahead! The key is to pause, consider the risks, and make a measured decision—because in the real world, unmitigated risks can cause damage like unforgiving asteroid fields.

But you also don't want to constantly broadcast, ***"I have a bad feeling about this,"*** throwing negativity into the atmosphere. That can become a self-fulfilling prophecy and sap team morale. If a leader lacks faith in succeeding, it's unlikely anyone else will run full speed through the metaphorical asteroid field.

Your job is to find balance: cultivate cautious optimism that inspires confidence without ignoring the potential for setbacks. Fortunately, risk management processes exist to help:

- Identify risks thoroughly.
- Estimate the probability and impact of each risk to prioritize efforts on high-impact, likely issues.
- Create a risk response plan tailored for each major risk, which could include:
    - Mitigate: Reduce the chance or impact. (Just as Han might turn on a shield or plot a careful course through larger asteroids, project managers can reduce risks by adding quality controls or extra resources.)
    - Avoid: Change plans to sidestep the risk entirely. (Han could have heeded C-3PO and taken another route, but that might have had other risks. In the project world, sometimes stepping back is wise—avoiding a risk entirely can save the team from unnecessary danger.)
    - Transfer: Outsource the risk or insure against it. (Like purchasing insurance or outsourcing a high-cost activity, transfer can reduce exposure—though Han's rebels couldn't pass that off.)
    - Accept Actively: Prepare contingencies or a backup plan. (If Han could have anticipated the asteroid field and planned alternatives, he probably would have, but he didn't have that luxury. In projects, we may choose to accept a risk and proactively create a backup plan.)
    - Accept Passively: Take a ***"wait and see"*** approach, as Han essentially did, relying on instinct and skill. Of course, he didn't have a choice. In the business world, for lower impact risks, we may choose to wing it and adapt.

- Turn Risk into Opportunity: Sometimes risks reveal hidden chances. Han's gamble worked, using the asteroid field to lose pursuers.

Regarding turning risks into opportunities, in one IT project, a company planned to roll out a new Customer Relationship Management *(CRM)* system across multiple regions. Early on, the team identified a major risk: integrating data from disparate legacy systems could cause delays and disruptive downtime. Instead of fearing that risk, they seized it as an opportunity to upgrade their integration processes and adopt automated tools. This not only avoided the original risk of delays but also improved overall data quality and streamlined sales and marketing workflows—adding unexpected value far beyond the project's initial scope.

One last tip: For uncertainties with wide ranges, the *Program Evaluation and Review Technique (PERT)* is useful. The weighted formula *(O + 4M +P) / 6 (where O = optimistic, M = most likely, and P = pessimistic estimates)* leans estimates toward the most probable outcome, balancing differing viewpoints—because projects often include the optimist, realist, and pessimist, each vital to a rounded view. The key is to base these different viewpoints on an actual list of risks *(and their impact and probability)*, not just a hunch.

A vivid Star Wars example illustrates where PERT could have made a difference: The Rebel Alliance's mission to destroy the Death Star in *Episode IV – A New Hope* was a complex, high-risk operation. Pilots had to navigate tight trenches, time their attack runs exactly, and coordinate actions precisely—all under uncertainty from enemy defenses and unpredictable events. If the Rebels had applied PERT, they could have mapped the whole mission as smaller tasks with optimistic, likely, and pessimistic timings, identified dependencies, and calculated the critical path. This would have helped them prepare contingency plans for delays or failures and better manage risks, taking the edge off pure luck and skill. While Han Solo relied on instinct to escape asteroid fields, managing a large, intricate operation like the Death Star attack calls for structured probabilistic planning—just like PERT offers in project management.

🎬 DIRECTOR'S COMMENTS

I was one of those 17-year-old kids waiting in line when Star Wars first came to the theaters, before all the prequels and sequels and spinoffs. I didn't know what to expect—all I knew was the title and that it had something to do with spaceships. I didn't realize I was at the forefront of what would become decades of cinematic lore that would entertain and inspire me, and countless others, for years. At its heart it was a space western for all ages, with heroes and villains galore, but it was also a vehicle for conveying timeless principles about life.

"Never tell me the odds" has become a personal mantra for me. I naturally assess risks and consider many angles, so when others say, *"You can't do this,"* I think of Han's bold refusal to be discouraged. I don't charge in blindly, but nor do I back away from challenges simply because the odds seem long. If I did, I never would have become a writer—the only guaranteed failure is not trying.

"I have a bad feeling about this" reminds me to avoid negative self-talk, but it also serves as an early warning system. Sometimes that feeling signals real concerns to address. After assessing risks rationally, though, I move forward without second-guessing. If it doesn't work out, I learn and adapt.

REALITY SHOW: WHEN LIFE IMITATES ART

These lessons have played out in my career in many ways:

I once led a large global IT program with a tight but feasible deadline, relying on strong communication and staged rehearsals. A bit of *"Never tell me the odds"* helped propel us, but detailed risk mitigation—including a homegrown web page for sharing updates—ensured I never had a real *"bad feeling."*

Years earlier, I led a doomed project with unrealistic deadlines, scarce resources, and a sponsor who kept changing the scope. My inner voice kept repeating, *"I have a bad feeling about this,"* but as a newbie, I went with the flow. The project finished late and over budget. The sponsor embraced a *"Never tell me the odds"* mindset, blindly rushing into what author Ed Yourdon calls a *"Death March."* A proper risk assessment—which I would've insisted on later in my career—might have saved us from flying straight into an asteroid field.

At a Harvard Club forum with CIOs and CFOs, the challenge was balancing perspectives. CIOs needed to explain in plain language why projects take time and money, detailing risks without sounding overly pessimistic. Meanwhile, CFOs, unfamiliar with technology jargon, wanted to move fast and lean. This required executives on both sides to reconcile their inner C-3PO and Han Solo—communicating risks clearly and finding common ground on a course of action without killing momentum.

Early in my career, when asked if something could be done, I was like Scotty from *Star Trek*, initially pointing out problems—*"We can't do it, Captain! We need more power!"* (Of course, good old Scotty always found a way in the end.) Now, inspired by *Star Wars*, I say, *"Anything can be done. It depends on time, money, scope, and how we manage the risks."*

It's a balancing act that takes practice and experience.

 "IT'S A WRAP!"

Whether you tend to throw caution to the wind or err on the side of caution, the next time you face a tough decision or challenging project, remember this: find the balance between *"Never tell me the odds"* and *"I have a bad feeling about this."* Assess risks carefully, weigh the pros and cons, and then confidently set your plan in motion. Charge into the galaxy with eyes wide open—and may the Force be with you!

🎬 PRESENTED BY...

JERRY MANAS, PMP

Jerry Manas is an internationally bestselling author, speaker, and consultant.

Jerry is frequently cited by leading voices in the world of business, including legendary management guru Tom Peters *(In Search of Excellence)*, who often references Jerry's bestselling work, *Napoleon on Project Management*, for its insights on simplicity and character, and Pat Williams, Senior VP of the Orlando Magic, who called Jerry's book, *Managing the Gray Areas*, *"a new path for leaders."*

His book, *The Resource Management and Capacity Planning Handbook*, was touted by Judith E. Glaser, noted author of Conversational Intelligence, as *"the first book dedicated to what is essentially the drivetrain of organizations—the effective use of its people toward its most important activities."*

Jerry's work has been highlighted in a variety of publications, including the Houston Chronicle, Chicago Sun Times, National Post, Globe and Mail, Huffington Post, and others.

When Jerry isn't in Projectland, he's probably in Bucks County, PA, with his wife and daughter looking at the back of his head while he writes, with Max the dog at his feet. Visit his website at www.jerrymanas.com.

CHAPTER 7

THE HONEST BROKER AND THE RULEBREAKER
Ghostly Secrets for Handling Difficult Executives *(Ghostbusters)*

GHOSTBUSTERS
Logline: "Three parapsychologists forced out of their university funding set up shop as a unique ghost removal service in New York City, attracting frightened yet skeptical customers."⁷

SETTING THE SCENE
THREE PARAPSYCHOLOGISTS ARE KICKED OUT OF THEIR UNIversity teaching positions at Columbia University after their research grant is terminated. It comes at a unique time, as New York City is being overrun by dastardly ghosts—some just playfully mischievous while others are hell bent on destroying civilization. Rather than wallow in the misery of losing their tenured jobs, they form The Ghostbusters on a low budget and with high hopes of thwarting the ghost and demon takeover of NYC. Business soon picks up, and a fourth Ghostbuster, Winston Zeddemore *(Ernie Husdon)* is hired.

In one scene, they are talking with the mayor of NYC about the fact that the city is heading for *"a disaster of biblical proportions."* When the mayor asks, *"What do you mean biblical?"* Dr. Raymond Stanz *(Dan Akroyd)* says, *"Old Testament, Mr. Mayor, real wrath of God type stuff. Fire and brimstone coming down from the skies. Rivers and seas boiling."* Dr. Peter Venkman *(Bill Murray)* adds, *"Human sacrifice, dogs and cats living together... MASS HYSTERIA!"* Both get the point across, albeit in significantly different ways.

> **HOT TAKE:** Both the voice of reason and the voice of hyperbole play a role in getting and then keeping the attention of the project owner.

THE MOVIE MOMENT

While there are multiple scenes that shine a light on Stantz and Venkman's differing personalities, one of my favorite examples is at the climax of the movie when our lovable busters of ghosts have one last chance to stop the destruction of the known world. They face a mighty battle with the shapeshifting goddess of chaos and destruction—Gozer the Gozerian *(Slavitza Jovan).*

There's an opportunity *(they think)* to open up a dialogue with her.

```
Stantz (our honest broker): "Gozer the Gozerian? Good
evening. As a duly-designated representative of the
City, County, and State of New York, I order you to
cease any and all supernatural activity and return
forthwith to your place of origin, or to the nearest
convenient parallel dimension."

Gozer: "Are you a god?"

    Stantz looks at Venkman (our rule breaker) who
        lifts a fist and nods to him to say yes.

Stantz: "No."

Gozer: "Then die!"
```

She then proceeds to hit them with her powerful demon-death-ray-laser-light show to try to kill them.

After getting blasted with lasers by Gozer and almost dying, we find out that Venkman isn't the only rule breaker of the group. While gathering themselves after almost being blown off the roof of the skyscraper by the Gozer lasers, one of the other Ghostbusters, Winston Zeddemore, says, *"Ray. When someone asks if you are a god, you say yes!"* Had Stantz taken the advice of the rule breakers, the result would have likely been very different.

🎬 "ACTION!!!" PROJECTLAND SUCCESS TIPS

I'm a huge dog lover and a rescue dog advocate—my pit mix, Bodhi, gets his name from Patrick Swayze's character in *Point Break*. Watching a documentary about dogs and their ancient bond with humans, I learned it all started when our ancestors lived in caves, constantly facing threats from wild animals. Wolves, ancestors of today's dogs, sometimes got kicked out of their packs, forced to survive alone. Imagine such a lone wolf spotting humans with fire and food and approaching them—a risky endeavor that broke its survival instincts. The human who accepted this wolf likely saw a potential protector, leading to the unique bond we now cherish.

In this story, the wolf represents the rulebreaker *(like Venkman from Ghostbusters)*, and the human the honest broker *(like Stantz)*. Without both—the risk-taker and the grounded mediator—we wouldn't have the incredible partnership that defines our best friends today.

Venkman and Stantz have a common goal—self-preservation while saving their beloved city, and each offers a different approach to get there. In Projectland, you will encounter rule breakers like Venkman, honest brokers like Stanz, and many other personalities and approaches. Unfortunately, you may also encounter difficult executives asking tough questions with no clear, correct answer. As you determine how best to navigate this wild world, and all of the creatures that you meet along the way, consider:

Success in Projectland requires leaders and team members willing to embrace uncertainty and unknown territory, as well as the courage to find the right path to reach groundbreaking and sustainable goals.

As you seek the right path in your version of Projectland, be willing to explore what the honest broker and the rule breaker would do. Always being the honest broker could result in your being viewed as naïve and ultimately slain in a cut-throat corporate culture. Always being the rule breaker could leave you in perpetual state of chaos and viewed as a loose cannon.

Whether you're asked a straightforward question, one that seems impossible to answer, or one that feels downright ridiculous, you will have to respond in some way. With an open mind and with a little help from your team, you may be surprised how often the ridiculous question leads to producing the most interesting solutions.

And perhaps the most important lesson is in projecting the right level of confidence at the right time. If someone in power who is threatening your world asks if you are a god *(i.e., if you've got this)*, would you say yes or no? Are you confident enough in your and your team's abilities to deliver the project successfully? Executives can smell fear. If you are not confident in yourself, why should they be confident in you?

📣 DIRECTOR'S COMMENTS

As a solopreneur who previously spent over twenty years in the perceived stability of the corporate world, this scene encapsulates my career journey. Every day I have to be the honest broker and the rule breaker.

In 1982, I was in the seventh grade. I was the Venkman rule breaker who was excited to put on football pads, so I could deliver hits and get hit more safely, all while being incredibly reckless. I was also the Stantz honest broker who went to the middle school dance with both the intention of asking a girl to dance and the knowledge that I would ultimately embody Young MC's lyric and *"stand on the wall like I was Poindexter."* And that is exactly what I did.

As an adult, there are some days where the honest broker needs to be more prevalent. For me, these are typically administrative days where the work is straightforward. For instance, follow-up emails, accounting, and reviews of keynote speaking contracts where any rule-breaking could find me on the receiving end of a proverbial Gozer The Gozerian's demon death ray laser light show.

On other days the rule breaker mindset is more helpful. Days like this tend to include inner monologues like, *"Chris, you must be crazy. There's such a rare chance this will work. But it only takes one person to say yes, so why not try?"* Things like crafting and sending emails to pitch myself to the biggest podcasts in the world as a guest. Or sending copies of my books to massive stars who've shown a proclivity for '80s pop culture in the hopes that it actually reaches them—and then with even more hope that they'll share it on their platforms. Or, submitting myself as a keynote speaker to huge conferences like SXSW and household name global organizations.

But most days are a battle of balance between my inner Stantz and Venkman, which is why I relate to this scene so much.

In the spirit of our brave Ghostbuster Winston Zeddemore, who reminds us that when someone asks if you are a god, the answer is *"Yes,"* I have grown from the boy too shy to ask a girl to dance into the man who believes in himself enough to say *"Yes,"* even when I'm asked to take on something I've never done before.

And this is exactly what brave project people do at the start of every project.

🎬 REALITY SHOW: WHEN LIFE IMITATES ART

This lesson showed up for me when I decided to leave the corporate world to become a keynote speaker and author.

I was in a job that wasn't working for me, and I was having a pity-party-of-one on my couch. I needed to find a new way forward in my life. A new career. A journey. But responsible adults can't leave a job and a career on the exact day of your personal epiphany, wing it, and hope something better will come along. I suppose you can, but it wouldn't be wise, which is where the honest broker came into play for me.

So, I wrote an article on problem-solving lessons from *The Breakfast Club* and got a huge and surprising response. Once I'd established that there might be something in this idea of writing lessons from 80s pop culture, I wrote and self-published a little book and taught myself how to build a website so I could also position myself as a speaker. All the while, the honest broker in me was reminding me to not do anything rash and keep my full-time job until I was positioned well enough to become the rule breaker and leave the corporate world for entrepreneurship.

As the months went on and I was thinking about writing a second book while using my Paid Time Off *(PTO)* for speaking gigs instead of vacation, the rule breaker was beginning to become the louder voice in my head. The honest broker was still telling me not to do anything spontaneous, but I knew that if I continued to only listen to the honest broker, I would continue to find myself in that **"life of quiet desperation"** that Henry David Thoreau talked about.

Eventually my inner rule breaker and honest broker made a deal. I set a timeline for leaving my full-time job. I devoted my whole self to chasing the dream of being a speaker and author. After 18 months of burning the proverbial candle at both ends, I followed the rule breaker right out of the corporate world after having invested over twenty years of my life there.

I made that Robert Frost **"two paths diverged in a wood, and I took the one less traveled"** decision.

From that day forward, I have sought a balance between the honest broker and the rule breaker. In the lyrics of Rob Base and DJ E-Z Rock, **"It takes two to make a thing go right,"** and I wouldn't have it any other way.

🎬 "IT'S A WRAP!"

Whether you are in a corporate position or taking the Cypress Hill *"insane in the membrane"* route of entrepreneurship as a consultant/freelancer like me, you are going to face situations where a project or situation feels like you are standing in front of the *"Gozer the Gozerian"* of project sponsors and you need to have the right answer.

And just like Gozer, they can choose to throw challenging roadblocks, micromanage you into oblivion, or train their minions on you. This is when you decide whether you are going to be the honest broker or the risk taker who takes the Winston Zeddemore approach—telling them you're a god and can handle anything thrown your way. While I'm kidding about telling them you're a god, having the inner self confidence to know that you and your team can tackle any challenge the project sponsor puts in front of you should absolutely make you feel powerful.

Being the honest broker like Stantz doesn't always mean that you and your team will get knocked down with a demon-death-ray-laser-light show. And being the rule breaker like Venkman or Zeddemore won't always mean that you'll get away with taking a fly-by-the-seat-of-your-pants monumental risk. The key is understanding the situation you're facing in that very moment and recognizing what is called for: the honest broker or the rule breaker. That choice may come from experience or it may come from that Magnum P.I. *"little voice inside you."*

Every project is different and every executive is different, so there isn't going to be a *"one size fits all"* approach. You may not always choose wisely. We humans aren't perfect, and our best learnings will likely come from our mistakes. Fortunately, *"it takes two to make a thing go right,"* so if you take the wrong approach and get knocked down, it probably won't be with a Gozer the Gozerian demon-death-ray-laser-light show. You'll still have another shot to get it right.

And one bonus nugget if you are contemplating a big change that encapsulates both the honest broker and the rule breaker, Johnny Cade in *The Outsiders* said, **"You still have a lot of time to make yourself be what you want."** Be honest with yourself about who you really are and be a big enough rule breaker to take a chance and show the world what you're made of.

🎬 PRESENTED BY...

CHRIS CLEWS – KEYNOTE SPEAKER, AUTHOR, 80'S POP CULTURE ENTHUSIAST

Growing up in the '80s and later spending over two decades in corporate marketing, Chris Clews discovered the perfect formula for his career: blending business and life lessons with the movies, music, and moments of the decade that shaped him. Today, he's a sought-after keynote speaker and author who shows audiences what *Ferris Bueller, The Goonies, and other pop culture icons* can teach us about work, leadership, and life.

Chris has shared his insights with organizations like VISA, Penn Medicine, DHL, Duke Health, and the University of Florida. He's also the author of the three-volume series *The Ultimate Series on Essential Work & Life Lessons from '80s Pop Culture*, featured in outlets such as Entrepreneur.com, *Esquire UK*, and on FOX, NBC, and CBS. A regular moderator for '80s pop culture panels—including cast reunions for *The Goonies* and MTV's original VJs—Chris brings enthusiasm, humor, and heart to every stage.

Passionate about giving back, Chris volunteers with animal rescues and donates a portion of his book and speaking proceeds to shelters. True to his favorite quote from Ferris Bueller, he believes that life moves pretty fast—and if you don't stop to look around once in a while you just might miss your next big lesson.

Learn more at chrisclews.com.

CHAPTER 8

FAIL FAST. LEARN FASTER. LEAD SMARTER.

How an Agile Astronaut Iterated His Way Home *(The Martian)*

The Martian
Logline: "An astronaut becomes stranded on Mars after his team assumes him dead and must rely on his ingenuity to find a way to signal to Earth that he is alive and can survive until a potential rescue."[8]

SETTING THE SCENE

MARK WATNEY (MATT DAMON) IS A BOTANIST AND ENGINEER on NASA's Ares III mission to Mars. When a powerful sandstorm forces the crew to abort their mission, Watney is struck by debris and presumed dead. The rest of the team evacuates Mars, leaving him behind, isolated, injured, and stranded millions of miles from Earth.

With no means of communication, limited supplies, and a habitat designed for short-term use only, he confronts the ultimate unexpected change in project scope. The mission is no longer to explore Mars. It's survival.

So, what does he do? He can't stick to the original plan. He can't wait for perfect information. Instead, he adapts and begins to tackle problems one at a time.

Watney adopts an approach that any Agile project leader would recognize:

- Identify the next immediate goal
- Assess available resources
- Test a solution
- Learn swiftly, adapt, and try again

From cultivating potatoes in Martian soil to generating water and restoring communication, Watney learns by failing fast and moving on to the next iteration, which pushes him to progress. His mindset is flexible, resilient, and focused on progress over perfection, serving as a model for anyone managing complexity, change, or crisis.

In true Agile fashion, he views uncertainty as part of the journey and not a barrier to success.

The Martian brilliantly illustrates Agile in action. Watney doesn't survive because he has a plan; he survives because he adapts when the plan fails. His iterative, experiment-driven approach is the ultimate project lesson.

HOT TAKE: When conditions change, address what's in front of you, learn quickly, and keep progressing one problem at a time.

THE MOVIE MOMENT

Shortly after patching himself up and accepting the reality of being stranded on Mars, Watney takes a breath, looks around, and delivers one of the film's most iconic lines: *"In the face of overwhelming odds, I'm left with only one option. I'm going to have to science the shit out of this."*

Watney's decision to "science the shit out of this" kicks off one of the film's most powerful story arcs: his desperate, ingenious attempt to grow food on Mars. This is a journey filled with trial, error, setbacks, and adaptation.

Gathering leftover potatoes from the crew's rations, he plants them in Martian soil, fertilizing them with vacuum-sealed human waste. It's grim, but effective.

When he realizes he doesn't have enough water to sustain the crop, he builds a system to generate it using rocket fuel and chemistry. His first attempt explodes, sending him flying across the habitat. He learns from his mistakes and tries again, ultimately keeping his potato farm alive.

Later, when a catastrophic structural failure destroys his entire crop, it's a huge blow. But Watney doesn't quit. He regroups, adapts, and presses on.

This entire potato rollercoaster is a brilliant example of Agile thinking under pressure: identifying the next most urgent problem, experimenting with solutions, learning quickly from failures, and constantly adapting to new challenges.

🎬 "ACTION!!!" PROJECTLAND SUCCESS TIPS

Watney's story isn't just about surviving Mars. It's a masterclass in Agile thinking under extreme pressure. He doesn't stick to a broken plan or wait for someone to save him. Instead, he gets on with it. He experiments and fails quickly. He learns even faster by adapting over and over again. That's the kind of mindset project professionals need when we're thrown into the unknown or dealing with shifting priorities, tight resources, or complex stakeholder environments.

What's powerful is how Watney simplifies his situation: What's the next immediate problem? What resources do I have? What can I try with what I've got? It's not flashy, but it's effective. A mindset of focused problem-solving is crucial for survival when everything feels like it's gone off course.

In real-world projects, this resilience and practical thinking can make the difference between spiralling into chaos and steadily finding a way forward.

In many projects, you don't need a detailed plan for the next six months. You need a way to make the next *move*. Progress in uncertainty is achieved through rapid learning loops, flexible thinking, and maintaining a mission-focused approach even when pressure intensifies. In other words, it is Agile at its best.

Watney teaches us:

- **Fail fast, learn faster**. Watney doesn't wait for a perfect solution. He tests, fails, understands, and keeps moving. In uncertain, innovative or complex projects, the speed of learning often matters more than accuracy.
- **Break problems down**. When faced with a massive challenge, focus only on the following problem. Solve that, then proceed to the next one.
- **Use what you've got**. Take stock of the available resources (however limited) and be creative, as constraints can fuel innovation.
- **Expect things to go wrong**. Build resilience into your mindset and planning. Recovery is an integral part of progress.
- **Stay mission-focused, not ego-focused.** Watney doesn't waste time complaining. He gets on with it one problem at a time.

That said, it's important to remember that not all failures are harmless. Watney's first attempt to create water ends in an explosion that nearly kills him. Agile thinking encourages rapid experimentation but also demands an awareness of risks. Failing fast should never mean failing recklessly. In real-world projects, balancing speed with safety and learning smartly, not just quickly, is critical when the pressure is on.

📣 DIRECTOR'S COMMENTS

The Martian is one of those films I go back to again and again, not just because it's entertaining, but because it's genuinely motivating. It's the kind of movie that fires me up, and the best part is that it's full of lessons we can apply to real life.

Yes, it's set on Mars, but it's a story about resilience and agility in the face of uncertainty. It's about solving problems under pressure, about doing your best work when everything's gone wrong and you're completely on your own. That, to me, is where it becomes deeply relatable, especially in Projectland.

There are times in project delivery, especially in high-stakes, high-pressure sectors like healthcare, when it genuinely feels like you've been left behind on another planet, armed with half a plan and barely enough resources to survive. The deadlines are brutal, the original scope has disintegrated, and somehow, all eyes are on you to figure it out and make it work.

What resonates with me is that Watney doesn't waste time panicking or pointing fingers. He focuses on what he can control, using whatever limited tools and information he has. He breaks the situation down, tackles each problem step by step, and when something fails, which it often does, he learns, adapts, and tries again. Throughout the film, we see his frustration. He gets emotional, and rightly so, but he never loses focus. He stays grounded, keeps moving forward, and even finds moments to laugh along the way.

That mindset, practical, resilient, and solution-focused, is one I've seen save projects. It's one I've had to adopt myself, especially in my environment where resources are tight, and scope can shift overnight due to new priorities, policy changes, or last-minute asks completely outside my control as a project manager.

In those moments, it's easy to feel overwhelmed, like you're trying to patch a hole in a boat with duct tape while the clock's ticking. But like Watney, you learn to breathe, step back, and focus on solving the next problem. You stop chasing perfection and instead aim for progress.

That's what gets projects over the line, not big heroic moves, but small, consistent, adaptable actions, even when the pressure is on.

And just like Watney, sometimes you've got to laugh not because things are funny, but because humor helps you stay human when everything else feels like it's about to break.

And let's be honest, that line, *"I'm going to have to science the shit out of this"*? That's the energy we all need when things go sideways in projects. It's funny, sure, but it's also quietly powerful. It says: I've got no guarantees. I've got limited tools. But I'm going to show up, try something, and move forward.

For me, *The Martian* reminds us that even when things fall apart, progress is possible: one creative decision, one brave test, one tiny win at a time. That's not just Projectland. That's life.

There's another reason why that line "I'm going to have to science the shit out of this" hits so hard. It's not just about determination, it's about the power of knowledge, expertise, and empirical thinking. Watney doesn't survive by guessing or hoping for the best. He survives by applying real scientific principles: testing, iterating, and trusting evidence over emotion.

In a world where science and expertise are sometimes undervalued or even dismissed, *The Martian* is a powerful reminder that real progress, whether on Mars or in a project environment, depends on critical thinking, grounded problem-solving, and respect for the knowledge that helps us adapt and survive.

🎬 REALITY SHOW: WHEN LIFE IMITATES ART

I've never been stranded on Mars, but I have been dropped into a project that felt close. It was a high-profile, high-pressure piece of work. The kind where expectations were sky-high, resources were thin, the budget was already stretched, and then, suddenly, everything changed. The scope shifted dramatically. Priorities were flipped overnight. The delivery team was restructured halfway through. And despite all that, the deadline didn't move.

The hardest part? No one really knew what was coming next. There was no precedent. No clear plan. Just a lot of ambiguity and a need to act fast. At times, it felt overwhelming like we were navigating in the dark, constantly adjusting to new challenges we couldn't have predicted. It was frustrating not having clear answers, but standing still wasn't an option.

Like Watney, we had to accept that the original plan no longer applied. We couldn't wait for perfect information or hope that things would settle down. Instead, we focused on what was right in front of us. What do we know? What's the immediate risk? What can we fix today?

As Mark Watney puts it in *The Martian*, "You solve one problem. And you solve the next one. And then the next. And if you solve enough problems, you get to come home." That became our approach.

One day, we were asked to create a new workflow to support a major process change with no notice and only 48 hours to turn it around. Another time, a set of national reporting requirements landed late in the day, with a deadline that left no room for traditional development cycles. We pulled together as a team, spun up a temporary dashboard using existing tools, and refined it live based on user feedback.

On more than one occasion, we had to rebuild deliverables from scratch because assumptions had changed upstream (i.e., in the earlier stages). We even redefined how stakeholders engaged with our program, replacing lengthy governance meetings with short, focused touchpoints to accelerate decision-making.

It was chaotic, imperfect, and often messy, but it worked. Personally, I learned to lean into the uncertainty rather than resist it. It taught me that progress wasn't about having the perfect answer upfront. It was about building momentum one small win at a time. Some days felt like patching holes in a leaky ship with duct tape, but we kept going because the alternative of giving up was never an option.

Looking back, it wasn't a perfectly planned project that got us through. It was Agile thinking, short feedback loops, iterative delivery, and the ability to pivot when the ground kept shifting beneath us. That project didn't succeed because we had certainty. It succeeded because we kept showing up. We tried, we failed fast, and we learned faster. Just like Watney. Just like the best project teams I've worked with.

If I could do it again, I'd remind myself even earlier that change isn't the enemy; rigidity is. Staying flexible, staying connected as a team, and staying focused on the next right step made all the difference.

🎬 "IT'S A WRAP!"

The next time your carefully crafted plan falls apart, when the scope shifts overnight, the timeline disappears while the end date remains fixed, or you're left trying to deliver with fewer tools than you need—don't freeze, don't panic, and don't wait for certainty.

Instead, work on the next problem.

Channel your inner Watney. Break it down. Solve the next thing in front of you. Fail fast, learn from it, and try again smarter this time. That's how real progress is made, especially in high-pressure environments where ambiguity is a given and perfection is a myth.

You don't need to be a rocket scientist to lead like one. You just need to be curious, calm under pressure, and committed to moving forward, one brave, practical step at a time.

Because when everything feels like it's gone off course, an agile mindset could be the difference between a failed project and a breakthrough.

🎬 PRESENTED BY...

JAMES EVANS

James Evans is a project professional, speaker and PMO leader who's spent his career helping people make sense of the chaos that often comes with delivering change. He holds a Master's degree in Project Management and has led complex programs across different sectors, learning that success is rarely about sticking to the plan—and almost always about how you respond when it goes off-script.

James regularly speaks at conferences and webinars, sharing honest reflections from the frontline of delivery. He also writes *Lessons Blogged*, a personal blog for project professionals where he explores the reality behind post-implementation reviews, from leadership wins to lessons learned the hard way.

He hasn't grown potatoes on Mars, but if you ever need someone to lead a rescue mission with limited resources, shifting priorities, and an unclear brief, James is probably your guy.

Beyond the spreadsheets and stand-ups, James is passionate about building epic teams through psychological safety, mentoring the next generation of project professionals, and helping others unlock their own project management superpowers. He leads with compassion, believes deeply in people's potential, and has a knack for spotting strengths others didn't even know they had.

When he's not in Projectland, you'll probably find him in Wales, out on the run, throwing punches in a boxing ring, buried in a good book, or catching the latest release at the cinema. He's a lifelong learner, a creative thinker, and someone who genuinely enjoys helping others thrive.

WITH YOUR VISION, STRATEGY, AND APPROACH SET, IT'S TIME TO BUILD AND LEAD THE PROJECT TEAM.

DISCOVER HOW FOSTERING TRUST, EMPOWERING OTHERS, AND SKILLFULLY MANAGING CONFLICT CAN INSPIRE TEAMS AND DRIVE COLLECTIVE ACHIEVEMENT IN ANY PROJECT ENVIRONMENT.

DIRECTING THE SHOW
LEADERSHIP & TEAMWORK

ACT II

CHAPTER 9

TEAMWORK AND TRUST IN MIDDLE-EARTH

Building Your Project Fellowship *(The Lord of the Rings: Fellowship of the Ring)*

The Lord of the Rings: The Fellowship of the Ring
Logline: "A meek Hobbit from the Shire and eight companions set out on a journey to destroy the powerful One Ring and save Middle-earth from the Dark Lord Sauron."[9]

SETTING THE SCENE

ELVES, UNDER THE GUIDANCE AND MANIPULATION OF SAURON, the embodiment of evil in Middle-earth, forged 19 powerful rings to be distributed across the land to help the Dwarves, Elves, and Men thrive . . . or so they thought. As it turns out, Sauron forged a 20th ring—*the One Ring to rule them all*—in the fires of Mount Doom *(a volcano)*. This all-powerful ring was to be used to rule over all the other rings and ultimately, turn the world into darkness. What a terrible deception! But who could rid Middle-earth of Sauron, the One Ring, and all the evil they bring?

That's where *the Fellowship of the Ring* comes into play. Through a series of adventures, the One Ring finds itself in the hands of Frodo Baggins *(Elijah Wood)*, a Hobbit. Hobbits are a small, happy race of beings who live in the countryside called the Shire. They're a simple and jolly folk—their time is spent farming, fishing, dancing, and drinking. Gandalf *(Ian McKellen)*, among the wisest of the wizards in Middle-earth, is a dear friend of Frodo and tells him about the One Ring and how it must be destroyed.

Through a series of both unlikely and inevitable events, Frodo and his companions Samwise, Merry, and Pippin wind up in Rivendell with the Council of Elrond. This Council is a group of Dwarves, Elves, and Men who lead Middle-earth and work together to keep it safe. Hobbits have not had representation on the Council and were never given one of the rings.

> **HOT TAKE:** There's no one person who carries a project. There's no one hero—in Middle-earth and in life. No matter what you see in the headlines, it always takes a team to accomplish amazing things.

THE MOVIE MOMENT

The members of the Council of Elrond have assembled to discuss how they are going to get the One Ring to Mount Doom, located in Mordor, to destroy it. However, everyone has a different opinion on how to proceed. Some believe that the One Ring shouldn't be destroyed—instead, they should be allowed to wield its power. Some are foolish enough to think they can destroy it with their weapons—Gimli even breaks his axe trying to smash it. Egos and emotions are at their peak.

Through all the commotion and arguments, a quiet, unexpected voice arises. Frodo, the Hobbit, speaks up.

"I will take it. I will take it. I will take the ring to Mordor. Though, I do not know the way."

Hobbits are simple, tiny, unassuming creatures who easily get overlooked, typically do not get involved with life outside The Shire, and are also not seen as courageous. Yet here's Frodo, who has never left the Shire until now, standing up and taking the lead. He has no idea where Mount Doom is or the magnitude of what he's volunteering for. But his love for his people has given him the courage to raise his hand to lead a mission for which he is utterly clueless. This unexpected and noble act inspires others to gather around him and the arguments to cease.

Each of the folks who stepped forward has special skills, strengths, and unique personalities.

Gandalf – a Wizard who guides their path and watches over everyone

Aragorn – a Man and the ultimate warrior and leader

Boromir – a Man who winds up corrupt from the power of the One Ring, but whose courage saves the lives of many Hobbits

Legolas – an Elf whose heightened senses and talents with a bow and arrow are unmatched

Gimli – a Dwarf whose brute strength and talents with an axe make him irreplaceable

Pippin and Merry – Hobbits, twin brothers who have a knack for getting into trouble and providing comedic relief, but are dedicated to helping Frodo

Samwise – a Hobbit, Frodo's loyal best friend who never leaves his side

Frodo – a Hobbit, the only one that could bear the One Ring

And so, the *Fellowship of the Ring*, a.k.a. The Project Team is born!

"ACTION!!!" PROJECTLAND SUCCESS TIPS

As illustrated in *The Fellowship of the Ring*, successful projects thrive on diverse skills, perspectives, and working styles. An effective leader must adapt their approach to recognize, support, and inspire their team's unique talents to achieve the best results.

Project leaders:

- Must recognize that a project needs a variety of skills, styles, and perspectives to make it successful.
- Need to adopt different ways to understand, appreciate, and motivate their team's unique talents to inspire them to do their best work.
- Should welcome leadership from unexpected places—sometimes the **"Frodo"** on the team is the one to step up and move things forward.
- Must unite the group behind a noble quest—a shared goal helps quiet egos and align even the most unlikely companions.
- Can turn conflict into momentum by channeling differing views toward creative solutions, much like the Fellowship transformed disagreement into action.
- Should pair wizards with warriors, elves with dwarves—balancing visionary skills, problem-solving, and determination across the team is essential to overcome obstacles.
- Need steadfast allies (**"Sams"**) for support during tough stretches—loyalty and encouragement are as vital as leadership or specialized expertise.

We've seen these tips play out time and again in our versions of Projectland.

🎬 DIRECTOR'S COMMENTS

We are big fans of this entire movie series. *The Lord of the Rings* is a trilogy and *The Hobbit* is another trilogy that takes place just before it. After each having watched the movies separately many times, we discovered that our local theater was running the *The Lord of the Rings* trilogy all in one day. So of course, we jumped at the chance to sit for 12 hours in the dark. There are countless lessons we could highlight, so let's discuss why we chose this particular movie moment.

At the core of every project success are talented project team members that must form a cohesive team and learn to work well together. Every character in *The Lord of the Rings* has a unique skill and approach. Each member of the team could contribute, but no one person could do everything alone. Aragorn was a strong leader, but he couldn't carry the One Ring. Gimli was a fierce warrior, but leadership wasn't his role. Frodo bore the One Ring, but he wasn't a fighter. That's why the Fellowship of the Ring needed *every* member to succeed. Their strengths complemented each other, making the journey possible.

So how could this relate to you? In our experience in corporate and volunteer project work and launching a business, we have encountered all the players in Middle-earth. Everyone has gifts that they bring to the table. It's important to know this when building a team, while keeping in mind that saboteurs may come your way. And no matter your role, being self-aware enough to know your own skills and personality quirks under pressure.

🎥 REALITY SHOW: WHEN LIFE IMITATES ART

LEADERSHIP AFFECTS EVERYTHING

In *Lord of the Rings*, there are two prominent wizards—Saruman and Gandalf. Each one has powerful influence over those around them. Unfortunately, each also has different goals and different ways of leading. Saruman wants to cast Middle-earth into darkness and fire, and rule by punishment and death. Gandalf wants to cast out all evil and bring light to Middle-earth by bringing the best out in all races through showing them love and respect.

But how does this relate to projects? Well, in projects, you are going to encounter all types of leadership styles. You also may be a leader yourself, so you need to know what type of leader you want to be. Let's discuss two different forms of leadership you could encounter.

In one organization I worked with, the dysfunction wasn't caused by the employees executing the projects, it came from the top. Leadership was misaligned, constantly shifting priorities and expecting employees to not only change what they were working on at the drop of a dime, but also make the impossible possible. That confusion trickled down, creating frustration and demotivating employees because they didn't know if what they were working on would be relevant in a month, a week, or even in a day.

Like Saruman, the main leader was powerful, but what made that leader even more powerful was the rest of the leadership team following his style. For instance, communication was unclear, and they spoke poorly of other teams, which set the tone that negative language was okay. When caught in situations like this, what do you do? You only have a few options, such as: try and change the company culture from the bottom up, make the best of it as-is, or leave.

In contrast to Saruman, I had the opportunity to work with a leader who reminds me of Gandalf. Like Gandalf, she brilliantly orchestrated the team, understanding that she couldn't do everything on her own. She recruited and hired the right people for each position, creating a strong, collaborative environment. Calm, humble, and extremely smart, she empowered her team to thrive.

Instead of dominating conversations and commanding orders, she listened deeply and encouraged differing opinions. While everyone knew how brilliant she was, she also openly shared her weaknesses and encouraged us to critique her work. Similar to Gandalf's knowledge of Middle-earth and all its history, she had a deep understanding of our industry, guiding us with ease and confidence.

Leaders like her are rare. Her presence inspired us to work harder and longer hours when needed. We were willing to go the extra mile because we knew our leader was with us, doing the same.

As a professional, you will likely work with different types of management, so it is important to understand how to collaborate with them, and, if necessary, recognize when it's time to leave. On projects, you need to understand the influence you have and the ripple effect of your actions. Your colleagues are always watching you.

Particularly if you are in a project leadership role, if you're not paying attention or not engaged in a call, team members see it and they may think, **"Why should I care if my leader doesn't?"** If you have a negative attitude, they pick up on it, and it may become normal for everyone to have the same negative attitude. On the flip side, when you're fully engaged, they engage. If you emulate humility and honesty, they will too. If you put in the effort, they will be inspired to work hard for and with you.

THE TEAM IS EVERYTHING

When you have a master like Gandalf orchestrating your team from the top, the project management job gets a lot easier. Even if they pull together the unique and diverse set of skills you need to execute a complex project, this doesn't mean the people management part of the job is without its challenges. The problem with having so many different personalities on the team is that to keep them all moving forward together, you must have different approaches for each personality. Here are a couple of examples of how I've dealt with the diverse players that resemble those in Middle-earth.

Frodo is not the typical hero you would expect in an adventure like *Lord of the Rings*. He's more interested in a second breakfast than picking up a sword. As a hobbit, he's not known for being fast, agile, passionate, or goal oriented. Rather, the most important skill that he brings to the table is that he is humbler than anyone else in the fellowship. As such, he was the only one who would be able to resist the One Ring's power long enough to bring it to Mt. Doom to destroy it. Because of this critical role, it was important for the rest of the team to rally around Frodo and protect him using their unique skills, so the mission could be completed successfully.

Not every real-life project has a Frodo, but the larger, more complicated ones definitely do. Sometimes they have several. The Frodo on your project team isn't the leader, or the career driven warrior who seeks success at all costs. The Frodo on your team is one who has that unique, special skill that he's absolutely committed to contributing no matter what happens. That's all he has to offer, but he's the only one who can do it.

I had an experience with a Frodo on one of my projects. He was the developer for an extremely complicated assembly enhancement we needed for a new product line introduction. He had years of experience in this particular product line. The new enhancement was wildly complex and required input from multiple engineering data sources. This was one of the most complex projects I had ever worked on, and naturally, it had a critical deadline. Our Frodo was characterized by his gentle, friendly, and hardworking nature. He had no career aspirations other than to do his best. To make sure that he could do just that, the team rallied around him. We made sure that his work was uninterrupted and we managed communications with him very carefully.

We kept track of questions we needed to ask and scheduled time to review them rather than *"dropping in"*. Because of his expertise, he was regularly consulted by other teams for guidance on their projects, so part of our job was to make sure that we redirected them to another team that had more capacity. We also made sure that he was able to take much needed vacation time to visit with his family in another country after he'd worked diligently on the project for over a year. These approaches to protect his time and energy, enabled him to bring his best to the project.

We're not always that lucky. Sometimes a Gollum finds their way onto your team.

BEWARE THE GOLLUM

Gollum is a creature that used to be a Hobbit, but because of his exposure to the One Ring, has become addicted to its power. He's extremely dangerous for the hobbits to work with, but because he knows the way to Mount Doom, where they must go to destroy the One Ring, they must work with him. He has critical knowledge that they need to make their mission successful. However, they also know that he's dishonest and has ulterior motives. He's not interested in helping them destroy the ring, he just wants to take it for himself, so he pretends to be helpful while waiting for his chance to take it.

In a real-life project, I would never choose to have a Gollum on my team, but you don't always have a choice when there's a person with a critical skill that you need. In cases like this, management will tolerate team members of poor character because they absolutely need those skills to get the job done.

On a software project to develop a purchasing module, a brilliant individual on my team developed a complex set of code that created sequenced orders for a critical, expensive component of the product we were manufacturing. Nobody else knew how to write or modify the code. He was also a textbook narcissist, with all the manipulative, self-serving, and downright dishonest characteristics that go along with it. I would have liked to have fired him, but we couldn't do the project without him.

Unfortunately, there aren't a lot of effective ways to deal with these necessary evil characters. The method I chose was to micromanage him, making it impossible for his dishonesty and conflicting goals to interfere with the success of the project. I had frequent meetings with him, monitored all his communications, and checked on his work frequently with other team members to make sure everything was still moving forward smoothly. In addition, I paired him with another developer, so that he was no longer the only member of the team who knew the details of the software.

You shouldn't have to spend this much extra time on somebody in a professional environment. I'd like to live in a world where you don't have to micromanage anyone, but the reality is that sometimes you do. In these cases, it's best to have an approach prepared so you're ready.

"IT'S A WRAP!"

We hope that you're in complete awe of how incredible *Lord of the Rings: Fellowship of the Ring* sounds, if you haven't already seen it. We could go on and on about the lessons from the entire trilogy, but we're going to keep this short and sweet.

No one person is the same and no one project is the same. That means for each project, you will need the right, diverse group of people to get it completed effectively and efficiently. Getting any diverse group of individuals to work together and play their part can be a challenge. To accomplish this, you must recognize and appreciate the uniqueness each individual brings to the team. That way, much like *The Fellowship of the Ring*, you too can lead even the most daunting project to success.

PRESENTED BY...

MICHAEL SCHAFER AND RACHEL MUSSELL

Michael Schafer and Rachel Mussell started volunteering for PMI together in 2021, and in the process of planning and executing many events together, including teaching an introductory Project Management class, they discovered they aligned on many levels—nerding out about project management, *Lord of the Rings*, and a desire to change peoples' lives for the better. After developing and delivering project & life management educational experiences on a volunteer basis, they decided to get serious about it and founded Back in the Box Consulting, LLC.

"Why 'Back in the Box'?" For years we've been told to **"think outside the box."** That sounds great until you try it and realize just how overwhelming thinking outside the box can be—our cognitive load is exhausted! By driv-

ing as much of what we do as we can into standard, repeatable, three-step processes *(okay, maybe four)*, we can engage the box in the back of our mind—our subconscious—to free the front of our mind for more worthy work. This is the magic of getting **"Back in the Box."**

A special note from Michael and Rachel:

To those who are reading this book, thank you. Thank you for supporting Dawn, Jerry, and all the incredible co-authors who had the honor of writing this book for you. We hope you're learning valuable project management lessons that will serve you throughout your career and that you're discovering some movies you'd like to watch for the first time or rewatch with a fresh perspective.

To Dawn, thank you for inviting us to a once-in a lifetime experience as contributing authors of this book. Thank you for being a wonderful friend and mentor the past few years. We are so blessed to know you.

Company website: backintheboxconsulting.com

CHAPTER 10

ENOUGH WITH THE QUESTIONS ALREADY!

Turning a Collection of Strangers into a Team (12 Angry Men)

12 ANGRY MEN
Logline: "The jury in a New York City murder trial is frustrated by a single member whose skeptical caution forces them to more carefully consider the evidence before jumping to a hasty verdict."[10]

SETTING THE SCENE

SET IN 1957 NEW YORK CITY, A BOY HAS BEEN ACCUSED OF murdering his father. The trial concludes and the jury of twelve men now must deliberate to determine the verdict. As usual, jury members are strangers to one another and must collectively find a way to come to a decision.

The deliberation appears to be heading to a speedy conclusion with the initial vote seemingly a unanimous guilty verdict until Juror 8 (*Henry Fonda*) votes… not guilty! What follows is a series of discussions and events that cause some of the jurors to start rethinking their position.

> **HOT TAKE:** When building project teams, don't jump to conclusions about your team members or their capabilities before you get to know them.

 THE MOVIE MOMENT

With an open vote of 11 – 1, Juror 8 is asked to share why he voted not guilty. He explains that he doesn't know if the boy is not guilty; however, with the boy's life on the line, the boy deserves to have a closer examination of the evidence. One by one, Juror 8 addresses questions from the other jurors to see if it's possible the boy is innocent. He also asks for future votes to be taken by a secret ballot. He says if a secret ballot is taken, and all 11 other jurors still find the boy guilty, he will switch his vote to guilty as well.

As you can probably guess, since this is a full-length movie, the secret ballot includes one other not guilty vote. The deliberations continue with other jurors feeling more comfortable raising questions as well. What follows is a series of questions to review the evidence and see if it's possible someone other than the boy could have committed the murder.

At first, it is Juror 8 who is asking all the questions, examining the evidence. Over time, the other jurors begin asking questions too. The back and forth of asking and answering questions allows us to learn more about each juror. We learn about personal and professional lives, hobbies and interests, and perhaps most importantly, motives for why they voted guilty.

In one dramatic scene, the murder weapon is presented. It is a switchblade knife with a unique dragon design on the handle. A shop owner testified the boy had purchased the knife and the owner had never seen a design quite like that before. With such a unique weapon used to kill the man, how could it be possible that someone other than the boy could have killed the man? In an intense exchange, the jurors argue, *"This isn't possible! The boy must have committed the murder!"* To the surprise of everyone, Juror 8 reaches into his pocket and pulls out a knife with the same design! He bought the knife at a pawn shop just a few blocks away from the murder. By questioning what appears to be so obvious, we may find that it's possible to have a different perspective.

In another scene we learn of the testimony from the man living below where the murder occurred. He testified that he heard the body drop, heard a scream from a woman across the way, and then got out of bed. He walked out of his room, to his front door and saw the boy running down the stairs, all within 15 seconds. Questioning if this was possible, Juror 8 recreates the movements. He imitates the man, who walked with a severe limp, slowly tracing the steps. The other jurors encourage him to walk faster so he speeds his pace. Juror 8 completes the walk and asks for the time. 40 seconds, not 15 as the man testified. Is it possible the witness didn't see the boy run down the stairs after all?

It is through questions and answers like these that the *"angry men"* ultimately shifted from polarized to critical thinking and produced a thoughtful outcome.

🎬 "ACTION!!!" PROJECTLAND SUCCESS TIPS

There are so many parallels we can draw from *12 Angry Men* to our own experiences as project leaders. Our teams are often a collection of strangers. Perhaps some members know one another, but often we pull resources from various departments who've never worked together. Typically, we're given instructions and a set of facts we must work with to drive our project forward. Our project experience is a collection of deliberations, with team members working to prove a point or encourage us to change our perspective. The project team, just as with the jury, must define working agreements, assumptions, and build relationships to reach the objective.

When I consider the soft skills required to lead teams successfully, I often think about negotiation, motivation, inspiration and emotional intelligence. Those outside our profession may consider our technical knowledge and capabilities such as building schedules, managing budgets, and producing status updates to be the foundation of a successful project management career. However, it is these four soft skills that were on full display in *12 Angry Men*, and are truly the bedrock of successful project leaders.

To be an effective negotiator, or motivator, we must also be curious. Juror 8 came to the deliberation with an open mind. He was curious about what was possible before accepting the facts of the case as absolute. The same can be true for us in leading project teams.

When you receive an estimate from one of your subject matter experts, do you blindly accept it, or do you ask questions? When you are given a status update from a team member, do you dig deeper? When you are presented with solutions from a vendor do you accept those or seek out alternatives? When your new team is formed, do you allocate time for members to learn about one another? Our role is to lead the team to a successful project outcome, but we aren't provided a perfect blueprint for how to get there.

Here are a few recommendations to improve your chances for success and build a strong project team:

- **Get to know your team members.** Build a short questionnaire to learn more about the team. Use team time to review responses and ask team members to share stories about the items they listed on the questionnaire.
- **Incentivize team participation and curiosity.** Build a team culture where asking questions is not only accepted, but expected.
- **Customize Recognition.** Recognize that not everyone is equally comfortable or responsive to the same stimulus. Some may be ok with public acknowledgement while others prefer a private moment of thanks for work well done.
- **Take Time for Team Building.** Include team building time within your project schedule. The 10-15 minutes of bonding will go a long way to team unity. This can be used to celebrate birthdays, milestones reached, or simply ask, ***"How was your weekend?"***
- **Be Humble.** Understand you may be leading the team, but you aren't required to have all the answers. Listen to your team and empower them to take action when necessary—even if in conflict with your direction, if they make an effective case. A few years ago, I was recruiting a new employee for our team at The PMO Squad. We narrowed the field to the top two candidates. I preferred one but my leadership team preferred the other. As owner of the company, I would have been well within my rights to go with my choice. However, I listened to my team, and we hired their choice. Several years later, that employee continues to be a valuable member of our team and I'm grateful for the guidance from my leaders who made the right call.

📢 DIRECTOR'S COMMENTS

For the past 12 years, I've been leading a project management consulting firm. Each client and every engagement is unique. At the start of every new client interaction, I feel like Juror 8. Our clients reach out to us and share a challenge or problem they need assistance solving. They explain the situation and share all the *"facts"* with us, but we understand we are hearing only their version of the situation, their testimony.

Our standard process is to go through a discovery period and ask a series of questions. This is typically when the new client tells us we don't need discovery because they already shared everything we need to know to solve the problem. While I trust the client has been truthful, I also know we must verify what they've shared.

We also use the discovery period to learn more about the client. For our team to help solve their problem, we must get to know them to earn their trust. We know that during our engagement there will be times we will need to negotiate or motivate their team. Without questions, we don't have any knowledge of their circumstances, and we will be limited in our ability to influence or motivate. Curiosity opens the door to investigation and exploration; to learning what is possible.

REALITY SHOW: WHEN LIFE IMITATES ART

Several years ago, I was leading a Project Management Office *(PMO)* in the healthcare industry. This was my first experience in healthcare, but I had multiple PMO leadership roles with past companies. The interview process to get the job was quite exhaustive. I believe there were 19 different people I met with from various levels of the organization! I'm sure I was asked over a hundred different questions during the interviews. The healthcare system was doing their best to get to know me before making me an offer.

In one interview, my future boss shared that he liked my previous PMO experience and, although I didn't have healthcare leadership, I could bring a new perspective to the health system. I was excited for the opportunity and ultimately, they made the offer which I accepted.

Here I was leading a new team in a new industry after relocating my family for the third time in five years. I was also a member of the IT Leadership Team along with the other Executive Directors who were also new to me. All the newness was a bit overwhelming, but I realized I needed to be curious to learn more about the people, processes, technology, lunch spots, culture, and how to get on my boss's good side. Most of my first month was spent asking questions. The questions led to more questions and more questions. Why do we do it that way? Who decided that was the best way to do this? How do we communicate that? Tell me more about the benefits of that process. When do we need to get that done?

I was hired for my PMO Leadership experience, but to be effective I needed to learn about my team, peers, and the organization. In most cases, our success is not determined by what we know but by who we know and how deeply we know them. The relationships we build and the knowledge we have about our teammates is a much more important factor for success.

Another example where curiosity played a pivotal role in my career came at the very beginning of my project management journey. I was a young professional working as a software consultant for an IT company. My role was to help our clients utilize our software to the fullest potential. This included providing training, hands on demonstration, and sharing tips and insights to help the users be as efficient as possible.

One of our clients had purchased a new module and my manager, Dennis, asked me, *"How is the project going?"* I was curious about this new word he used and asked Dennis, *"What's a project?"* I had never heard of a project before. Project Management wasn't a subject covered at my college and none of my previous bosses had ever discussed a project with me in the past.

Dennis shared more about projects and project management with me. The more he shared the more interested I became. I started to do some research. Unfortunately, that was before we could *Google it.* Eventually, I enrolled in a continuing education course at Georgia Tech to learn more about project management. From that moment on, I've been hooked. I could have just moved on from Dennis's question and not been curious to learn more. Had that been the case, what a different life I would be leading today! From the very start of my time in project management, being curious has been at the center of my journey.

"IT'S A WRAP!"

For each project you lead, take the necessary time to be curious and learn about your team members. Create a safe space within your project team allowing curiosity. Build a team culture that encourages questions and empowers individuals to validate what may or may not be accepted as fact.

PRESENTED BY...

JOE PUSZ, PMO JOE

Joe Pusz is also known as *"PMO Joe"* and is an internationally recognized leader in the Project Management and PMO community. He is a frequent Keynote Speaker, Author, Project Management Innovator and creator of the *Purpose Driven PMO* and *Organizational Project Delivery Journey*. Joe speaks globally on Project Delivery, Leadership, PMOs, Purpose Driven Mindset, and other trending Project Delivery topics.

Joe is Founder and CEO of the award-winning firm, The PMO Squad, which is the #1 Project Management Staffing & Consulting firm across the entire United States in the 2024 Inc. 5000 list.

In addition to his role as CEO of The PMO Squad, Joe is the host of the Project Management Office Hours Radio Show and Podcast. He is Co-Founder of VPMMA, the Veteran Project Manager Mentor Alliance. He is the Founder of The PMO Leader global community and a Founding Partner of International PMO Day.

Joe continues to support the global Project Management Industry serving as a Judge for the Global PMO Awards, volunteer for the Global Project Management Forum, and is a long-time member of the Project Management Institute. He is a PMP & PMO-CP, PMI Volunteer, Sponsor, and Mentor.

CHAPTER 11

LEAD LIKE A WARRIOR

Unlocking Team Power for Breakthrough Success *(Wonder Woman)*

Wonder Woman (2017)
Logline: "When a pilot crashes and tells of conflict in the outside world, Diana, an Amazonian warrior in training, leaves home to fight a war, discovering her full powers and true destiny."[11]

SETTING THE SCENE

SET DURING WORLD WAR I, *WONDER WOMAN (2017)* FOLLOWS Diana Prince/Wonder Woman *(Gal Gadot)*, who leaves her sheltered island home of Themyscira after meeting American pilot Steve Trevor *(Chris Pine)*, whose plane crashes near the island. From him, Diana learns of the global conflict ravaging the outside world. Believing it to be the influence of Ares, the god of war, Diana feels it is her duty to intervene and bring peace. Armed with her shield, sword, and the magical Lasso of Truth, she travels with Steve to Europe and quickly finds herself thrust into the brutality of trench warfare.

This film blends mythology with history, framing Diana as both a fierce warrior and a compassionate leader who must balance her extraordinary powers with an understanding of humanity's struggles. Alongside Steve and a diverse band of allies— including Sameer, Charlie, and The Chief—she learns that victory comes not only through strength but also through teamwork. Her journey is not just about defeating villains but also about inspiring hope, building trust, and empowering others to rise above fear. But wait—we cannot forget the lovely Etta Candy, Steve's secretary! She is, after all, part of the team as well. While she may be in the background, we must acknowledge all the coordination and organization that she does for the group. *Everyone* plays an important role in getting the mission done!

> **HOT TAKE:** Leadership isn't about having all the answers or doing everything yourself. It's about empowering the team, making bold decisions, and creating the conditions for everyone to succeed.

THE MOVIE MOMENT

I love a good action movie that can depict and encompass chaos and challenges that ultimately result in reaching their goal and overcoming the obstacle. And yes, it will definitely capture my interest if there is a woman leading the way! There are two iconic scenes that highlight Diana's leadership style: the No Man's Land breakthrough, where Diana steps forward when no one else will, and the Village of Veld sniper standoff, where collaboration and improvisation turn the tide. These moments show how she embodies courage and conviction while rallying others to achieve what seemed impossible.

Scene 1: No Man's Land. Diana defies orders and charges across a deadly battlefield with her shield, drawing enemy fire so her team and allied soldiers can advance. In this scene, Diana Prince, Steve Trevor, and the rest of the small team are on the battlefield frontlines along with other American soldiers who are pinned down by German enemy fire. Diana and Steve are in a heated discussion where she wants to move forward so they can help the people suffering from the war, and he argues that is not their mission. In addition, they are outnumbered and outgunned and that is why *"no man"* has crossed over. Feeling the dire pressure and running out of time, she ultimately makes the executive decision to run out ahead with her shield and take on the heavy artillery coming their way so that her team, along with the rest of the American soldiers, can advance forward and gain the advantage.

Scene 2: The Village of Veld. When Charlie, the team's sharpshooter, freezes during a post-traumatic stress disorder *(PTSD)* episode, the group comes under intense fire in the Village of Veld. A German sniper high in the bell tower begins cutting down soldiers, and with Charlie unable to act, the mission seems doomed. In a split-second decision, Steve directs the others to drag a steel plate forward, creating cover for Diana. Seizing the moment, she launches herself into the tower, demolishes the sniper's perch, and secures victory. Their improvisation, and Diana's fearless charge, turn the tide, liberating the village and proving the strength of their unity.

> *"A piece of spaghetti or a military unit can only be led from the front end."*
>
> — General George S. Patton, Jr.

These moments show how a great leader leads from the front, adapts in real time, and brings out the best in others. Project leaders can succeed by focusing on the team's collective performance, not individual heroics.

"ACTION!!!" PROJECTLAND SUCCESS TIPS

Here are five Projectland Success Tips inspired by Wonder Woman:

Heroes Don't Lead Alone - recognize and recruit talent. Like Diana with her diverse, cross-functional team, identify each member's strengths and weaknesses.

The Art of Leading Boldly - lead from the front. Be the one who sets the pace and inspires others to follow—not by pushing but by pulling them forward, building trust amongst your team.

Courage in Action - adapt under pressure. When plans fail, encourage creativity and collaboration to find alternative solutions, especially when working with cross-functional teams.

Stronger Together - empower the overlooked. Even *"background"* contributors like Etta Candy prove that no role is too small in a project's success.

Lasso of Leadership - stay true to your tools. Your project leader's *"lasso, sword, and shield"* are integrity, knowledge, and dedication—leaders need their own tools and to hone their skills as much as their teams.

DIRECTOR'S COMMENTS

THE NO MAN'S LAND MINDSET

As a child, I grew up watching the original Wonder Woman *(played by Lynda Carter)* in the 1970's television show and always loved what she represented—a strong, compassionate, beautiful woman who fought for justice and defended those who could not fight for themselves. Then, more than 40 years later, Wonder Woman hit the big screen with this movie. In both the TV show and in the movie, she is underestimated and practically dismissed by most of the men she encounters, simply because she is a woman. It isn't until that pivotal moment in the No Man's Land scene that her courage and conviction is on full display. Diana doesn't wait for permission—she leads with action, and her boldness inspires the entire army to move forward.

As a Latina woman in the military, a male-dominated environment, I have had to face on numerous occasions, males challenging my authority. I also have had to deal with this issue as a project manager when faced with stakeholders' doubts on what I bring to the table. I have had to trust my instincts, step forward first, and show the way. True leadership is about stepping up and modeling the behavior you want to see in your team.

These experiences can happen to anyone, and I am sure you can think of a situation where you were faced with doubt. Perhaps like Diana, there was uncertainty as a new leader in a group, and you had to come up with a strong strategy to assert yourself as well as win the trust of the group. More importantly, you have a responsibility to trust in your team and expect that not everything will go according to plan every single time.

A good example that teaches this is the mindset of *"fail fast, fail often, fail forward."* I first saw this written on a whiteboard in a former boss's office. She lived by that mantra, which encourages resilience through failure and responding quickly to setbacks. This concept was originated by Carol Ann Bartz, former president and CEO of Yahoo!, and former chairperson, president, and CEO at architectural and engineering design software company Autodesk, in a speech she gave at Stanford University. This business mantra was heralded by Silicon Valley. While the idea *leans (see what I did there?)* toward Agile methodologies, Amy C. Edmundson, Harvard Business School professor of leadership, adds to this concept of focusing on failing intelligently.

> *"Intelligent failures are usually the result of efforts to learn or try something new that one can't possibly do perfectly the first time."* [12]
>
> — Amy C. Edmundson

Edmunson proposed three steps to ensure you are not just failing fast and often, but that you are also failing intelligently and learning from it, leading yourself to success: *Frame the Work*, *Invite Participation*, and *Respond*

Productively. Learning to pick your battles is key, especially when there are many risks involved and you need to determine the level of impact each will have on the project. As in the **"No Man's Land"** scene, Diana quickly assessed that she had to take swift action and charge forward to make way for the American army to stop the continuing suffering and loss of life.

Learning from failures is not about asking who or why, but *what*. It is tempting but not useful to point fingers and throw the blame on someone or linger to find out why something happened. Instead, get to the root issue of *what* caused it and learn from it. In the **"Village of Veld"** scene, Diana, Steve and the rest of the team improvised another solution to take out the enemy sniper. They figured out *what* to do. There was no time to blame Charlie or get upset with him when he could not fulfill his role at that critical point. Shifting your mindset from blaming to learning will aid in approaching failure collectively and finding alternate solutions.

Edmundson also suggests making sure the people around you feel comfortable speaking up. Creating an environment where people feel psychologically safe encourages them to speak up when they notice potential mistakes. Cultivating this atmosphere can help you avoid various types of unnecessary failures. After victory is reached at the Village of Veld, Diana and her team are assessing the aftermath of the ordeal they just faced. She points out to Steve what happened to Charlie, but she never calls him out on his failure; instead, she begins to understand his personal dilemma. Another key point is that the rest of the team also do not turn on him, instead choosing to come together to comfort him and celebrate their win. Accept the fact that at any given time, you or your team will make mistakes. Creating that safe space within your circle allows your team to share constructive feedback and hold honest conversations without fear of retaliation. Lead with your **"Lasso of Truth"** to build trust among your team and they will follow you into battle and fight alongside you.

🎬 REALITY SHOW: WHEN LIFE IMITATES ART

FROM BATTLEFIELDS TO BOARDROOMS

Throughout my military and civilian career, I feel fortunate that I have led many types of projects and teams consisting of various sizes, timelines, and budgets. Having read numerous books and articles on management and leadership, as you may have done as well, reading and experience tend to be confused as the same thing. But those of us who are more *"seasoned"* know they are two distinct concepts. Here are a couple of examples in my experience where I remember asking myself, **"Geez, if I only knew what I know now, that probably could have turned out better."** Live and learn, right?

The first example takes place during the tail end of my military service while the U.S. was in conflict with Afghanistan during Operation Enduring Freedom. I was the flight chief *(department manager)* for the Nutrition and Dietetics section, and our department was involved in standing up a brand new, top-of-the-line, Aeromedical Staging Facility *(ASF)*. We were the only hospital with this capability in the National Capitol Region. The ASF's sole purpose was to be the main hub that received all Wounded Warriors returning from overseas and provide top-tier medical care. The ASF would be their first stop back on American soil after a year or more since they were deployed.

Our role was to provide high quality, gourmet, hot meals to these patients. Being faced with a high-stakes deadline and conflicting priorities while balancing our current workload with an additional meal delivery system hindered the team's momentum. Like Diana's team in the Village of Veld, our *"expert"* froze. Without a backup plan, we risked failure. Channeling Wonder Woman, I encouraged brainstorming, pulled in other team members, and together we improvised a creative workaround. If I had not stepped up, the project might have stalled. As I mentioned in the Projectland Success Tip, *The Art of Leading Boldly*, leading from the front means being willing to take that first step so your team feels safe to follow.

A second situation came as a civilian contractor during a critical technology project when a key team member froze during a high visibility client demonstration. Similar to Charlie's hesitation in the Village of Veld, this lapse could have derailed our progress. Instead of focusing on what went wrong, I pulled in other team members, adjusted the flow, and encouraged collaboration under pressure. We salvaged the meeting and still delivered value to the client. This moment showed me the importance of another Projectland Success Tip, *Courage in Action,* adapting under pressure, encouraging creativity, and avoiding blame so the team can succeed together.

Another example was when a junior analyst, often overlooked, stepped up during a major deliverable. Their organization and documentation skills—usually in the background—became the key factor in helping us hit a critical deadline. It reminded me of Etta Candy's role—someone who is not always in the spotlight but vital to the team's success. Afterward, I made a point to highlight their contributions to leadership and the rest of the team. This reinforces the Projectland Success Tip *Stronger Together*, which highlights how empowering and acknowledging overlooked contributors is essential for morale and long-term team performance.

For additional tips and insight on team building, I highly recommend you read Dawn Mahan's book, *Meet the Players in Projectland*. This concept is covered in depth in Chapter 8 – *The Dream Team: The Fast, The Strong, & The Furiously Fun*.

"IT'S A WRAP!"

BEYOND THE LASSO: PROJECT LEADERSHIP LESSONS HIDDEN IN WONDER WOMAN

In Wonder Woman, Diana Prince shows us that effective leadership is not about being the strongest but about empowering the team to be stronger together. The next time you face your own **"No Man's Land,"** remember: Pull the team forward with courage, creativity, and where team-focused leadership is the path to project success.

If you're the project manager, there will be many circumstances you will encounter. You are looked upon as a leader. You are the liaison between the stakeholders, product owners, sponsors, and team members, and you will get bombarded with their issues, concerns, and complaints. You'll need to make hard, fast decisions on what the priority is at the moment and reduce or eliminate the obstacles you're facing to move the project along.

Whether we are fortunate to build our own team or inherit one, we all want the best players. But there are also times when you have to do your best with the resources you have. And so, as the great project manager you are or aspire to be, it is your responsibility to get to know your people; they are the backbone of the operation. You need to know their strengths, weaknesses, and areas of improvement for the team as a whole in order to know what skills you are working with. And just as important, the project manager also must hone their own skills and tools. Project managers may not carry a literal sword, shield, and Lasso of Truth like Wonder Woman, but we do figuratively have these tools represented as our integrity, knowledge, and dedication. In this way, we can stay true to our values and get the mission completed. Remember to stand, inspire and lead—strike your best heroic pose, grab your shield, and charge forward. Are you ready for the challenge?

 PRESENTED BY...

MARIE VILLEGAS

Marie Villegas is a retired Air Force active duty veteran and is currently working as an IT Senior Project Manager within the intelligence community. She earned an undergraduate and three graduate degrees specializing in business management, business administration, and IT informatics, as well as being certified in Project Management Professional *(PMP)*, Certified Scrum Master *(CSM)*, and Information Technology Infrastructure Library *(ITIL)*. She is passionate about connecting leadership lessons from pop culture to real-world project management. Marie enjoys building strong teams, mentoring new leaders, and yes, watching movies for inspiration!

She embraces the various challenges that each experience brings and turns them into highly useful golden nuggets of knowledge to not only strengthen her skillsets but those of her teammates. She has always loved what Wonder Woman represented and used that as a foundation to develop her leadership and management styles. As an avid reader, she is an aspiring author and humbly welcomed the opportunity to contribute to this book, combining these two loves into what she hopes becomes an inspiration and a teachable moment to the reader.

When she is not out playing the superhero at work, she looks forward to any opportunity to disconnect from technology and can be found on her deck reading a book from her endless TBR *(To Be Read)* list. And when she is feeling like a social butterfly, she is spending quality time with her family in New York and friends in Washington, DC, or off planning her next travel adventures across the U.S. and overseas. Connect with Marie at www.linkedin.com/in/marie-villegas1.

CHAPTER 12

LEADERSHIP IN THE FACE OF FEAR

How Ripley went from Survivor to Strategic Leader *(Aliens)*

Aliens (1986)
Logline: "Decades after surviving the Nostromo incident, Ellen Ripley is sent out to re-establish contact with a terraforming colony but finds herself battling the Alien Queen and her offspring."[13]

SETTING THE SCENE

HEROES AND HEROINES AREN'T BORN—THEY'RE SHAPED BY their experiences, their fears, and their ability to push through failure to find triumph. The road to greatness is rarely smooth. It's full of obstacles, tough decisions, and moments of doubt that require courage to move forward.

This process is at the heart of Joseph Campbell's *Hero's Journey*, a storytelling framework that highlights the universal path of growth and self-discovery. For project managers, this isn't just a storytelling device, it's a reflection of our reality.

Troubled projects from the past can stick with us: missed deadlines, broken trust, or plans that went off the rails. Those memories can linger, making us question ourselves and hesitate when new opportunities arise.

Ellen Ripley's story fits this framework perfectly. Each step of her journey in *Alien (1979)* and *Aliens (1986)* reveals new layers of her strength and resilience.

At the start of *Alien*, Ripley is just a third officer on the *Nostromo*, focused on her job: following protocols, keeping things running, and avoiding unnecessary risks. But when her crew picks up a distress signal, she's thrown into what Campbell calls the **"Call to Adventure."**

Her journey isn't just about surviving external dangers—it's also about betrayal. When Ripley insists on following quarantine rules to protect her crew, her authority is overridden. That one decision sets off a chain of events that costs lives.

If that wasn't bad enough, Ripley later discovers that Ash, the science officer, is secretly working for the sponsoring company. His orders? Bring the alien back to Earth at any cost—even if it means sacrificing the crew.

Ash's betrayal cuts deep, not just because it's dangerous but because it's a reminder that leaders sometimes must deal with sabotage and dishonesty from within their own team.

It's a brutal lesson in trust and survival that forces Ripley to rely on her instincts and resourcefulness. By the end of the film, she's transformed into the lone survivor, no longer just following rules but charting her own path to stay alive.

Fast forward to *Aliens*, and Ripley faces another defining moment. After waking up 57 years later, she's haunted by nightmares of what happened on the *Nostromo*. She's still carrying the weight of losing her crew, and now she's thrust into a world that's moved on without her.

When the Weyland-Yutani Corporation asks her to return to LV-426—the site of her trauma—as a ***"Civilian Consultant,"*** Ripley's first response is no. She doesn't trust them, and for good reason.

They assure her it's just an exploratory mission, but she soon finds out their real goal: to recover the aliens as biological weapons. Burke, the corporate representative, epitomizes this betrayal, quietly plotting to use Ripley and the team as pawns to secure his profits.

Despite all this deceit, Ripley rises above it. She faces her fears, chooses to protect others, and ultimately becomes the leader the team desperately needs.

> **HOT TAKE:** True leaders aren't fearless – they're forged through fire. Ellen Ripley didn't wait for permission. She took command when no one else would.

Ripley's journey across these two films is a powerful example of resilience. She shows us that our past doesn't have to hold us back, it can prepare us for what's next. Her story is a reminder that leadership isn't about being fearless; it's about finding the strength to push forward, even when everything around you feels uncertain.

 THE MOVIE MOMENT

Let's take a look at the following scene *(Script excerpt from IMDb: Aliens (1986) - William Hope as Lieutenant Gorman - IMDb)*

Lieutenant Gorman: *[to Apone over the mic while the aliens are attacking the marines]*

I want you to lay down a suppressing fire with the incinerators and fall back by squads to the APC, over.

Sergeant Apone: Say again? All after incinerators?

Lieutenant Gorman: *[irritated]* I said I want you to lay down a suppressing fire with the incinerators and fall back by squads to the APC...

[an alien sneaks up behind Apone and attacks him, his screams heard over the mic while his video feed goes dead]

Lieutenant Gorman: Apone... talk to me. *[more insistent]*

Lieutenant Gorman: Apone, talk to me...

Ripley: He's gone! Get them out of there! Do it now!

Lieutenant Gorman: Ripley, what the hell are you doing?

The hive ambush in Aliens is a moment of chaos, fear, and critical decisions—where leadership is tested, and the true leader emerges.

The Marines, confident and heavily armed, march into the hive with their weapons at the ready. At first, it seems like a simple search-and-rescue operation. But as they move deeper into the eerie, sticky corridors, it becomes clear they've walked into a death trap.

The Xenomorphs strike suddenly, emerging from the walls and ceilings in a flurry of acid and claws. Panic sets in almost instantly. Flamethrowers ignite randomly and bullets ricochet off walls.

Back in the APC *(Armored Personnel Carrier)*, Lieutenant Gorman—safely removed from the action—watches everything unfold on his monitors. The horrifying scene paralyzes him. He stammers, trying to issue commands, but his voice is shaky and uncertain. The Marines, hearing nothing useful, grow increasingly disoriented.

Ripley is sitting next to Gorman, watching the monitors as everything falls apart. She can't believe Gorman's inability to act. ***"Do something!"*** she shouts at him, her voice sharp with urgency. But Gorman freezes, his hands hovering uselessly over the controls.

That's when Ripley decides enough is enough.

She unbuckles her harness, jumps into the driver's seat of the APC, and slams the vehicle into gear. ***"Get them out of there!"*** she yells into the comms, her voice cutting through the panic.

The APC roars to life, barreling through the hive's narrow corridors. Ripley crashes through walls and alien corpses alike, plowing her way toward the Marines.

Inside the hive, Hicks, Vasquez, and Hudson hear Ripley's commands and rally to her position. Hicks, the most level-headed of the group, begins organizing the retreat. Vasquez, ever the fighter, lays down covering fire as the team moves toward the APC. Ripley expertly maneuvers the vehicle to create an escape route, keeping the Xenomorphs at bay with the APC's automated defenses.

Once the surviving Marines are onboard, Ripley slams the accelerator, racing out of the hive as Xenomorphs swarm the vehicle. Acid blood sprays across the exterior, sizzling against the armor. She weaves through the chaos, narrowly avoiding destruction, and finally bursts free of the hive.

As the APC speeds away, the team has a moment to breathe. The survivors—Hicks, Vasquez, Hudson, and even the android Bishop—look at Ripley with a newfound respect. She's no longer just the ***"civilian consultant"*** brought along for her knowledge of the Xenomorphs. She's proven herself to be the leader they need.

🎬 "ACTION!!!" PROJECTLAND SUCCESS TIPS

HOW RIPLEY DEVELOPED THE INFLUENCE TO LEAD

Ripley didn't start this mission with the team's trust, but this moment solidifies her as a leader. Here's how she earned their influence:

- **Seizing Initiative in the Face of Inaction:** Ripley doesn't wait for Gorman to regain control. By stepping into the leadership vacuum, she saves lives and prevents the situation from spiraling further.

- **Providing Clarity in Chaos:** Her calm yet authoritative voice over the comms cuts through the panic, giving the remaining Marines a clear direction to follow.
- **Building Trust Through Action:** Ripley doesn't demand respect—she earns it. By prioritizing the safety of the team and leading by example, she cements her place as the mission's leader.

DIRECTOR'S COMMENTS

I've been on my share of tough projects—the kind that keep you up at night, replaying every decision and misstep. Those experiences leave their mark: doubts, imposter syndrome, and the fear of stepping into high-pressure situations again.

No, I haven't faced the trauma Ripley endures in either movie, but her story resonates deeply. She isn't fearless, she's haunted by her past. Yet, when the moment calls, she doesn't let fear stop her. She steps up—not because it's easy, but because it's necessary.

What I admire most about Ripley is her focus on what matters: the people. In the hive ambush, when chaos erupts and Gorman freezes, Ripley doesn't waste time on rank or protocol. She takes control, drives straight into danger, and pulls her team to safety. It's not about ego or rules, it's about humanity.

By the end of *Aliens*, Ripley isn't just a survivor; she's a protector, a fighter, and a leader. She reminds us that leadership isn't about being fearless or perfect. It's about showing up, putting your team first, and acting with courage and compassion, even when the stakes are high.

Her story reminds me that scars from the past don't define us—they prepare us. True leadership is using those lessons to guide others toward something better. That's the kind of leader I strive to be.

REALITY SHOW: WHEN LIFE IMITATES ART

When I think about Ripley's bravery in the hive ambush scene in *Aliens*, it reminds me of my time working in disaster recovery after Hurricane Katrina. Like Ripley driving the APC straight into chaos to save her team, I found myself on the front lines of *The Road Home* program, helping people navigate the overwhelming bureaucratic maze to access the federal funds they needed to rebuild their lives.

The hurricane struck in August 2005, but *The Road Home* program didn't officially launch until July 2006. I joined the program in November 2006, initially expecting it to be a short-term opportunity. Little did I know I would spend the next eight years there, working across three different contracts. At the time, state contracts were limited to three years in duration. This meant that along with navigating the complexities of the program and the intense emotions of the people I was serving, I also faced the personal challenge of job insecurity. Each contract renewal brought uncertainty—there was no guarantee I'd be part of the next iteration of the program. Many colleagues who started with me didn't make the job cut when contracts changed, and the fear of losing my job was a constant companion.

Despite these challenges, I knew the work mattered. We were tasked with building everything from scratch—policies, processes, and systems—while onboarding and training a growing team to meet the overwhelming demand. Each day, I was reminded of why we were there. The residents we served had endured one of the most traumatic experiences of their lives, and their stories fueled our determination to find solutions, even when the path forward wasn't clear.

One of the greatest lessons I learned during this time was the importance of managing up. There were moments when I had to educate the very leaders running the mission, advocating for simpler policies and processes that prioritized the needs of the people we were serving over bureaucratic red tape. It took courage to stand up to those at the top, but it was necessary to ensure we could deliver the help our community needed.

Like Ripley in the hive, I had to cut through the chaos and focus on what truly mattered. Her bravery in facing the unknown resonates deeply with me, as does her reminder that leadership isn't about rank—it's about stepping up when it counts. It's about acting decisively, advocating for what's right, and finding strength in the face of adversity.

Looking back, my eight years with *The Road Home* program were foundational to my career in project management. I didn't recognize it at the time, but those experiences taught me resilience, adaptability, and the power of clear communication. They also taught me how to thrive in uncertainty, managing not only the fear of losing a job, but also the responsibility of serving those who had lost so much more.

Like Ripley, I learned that courage isn't the absence of fear—it's the determination to move forward despite it. Those lessons continue to shape how I approach every project and challenge in my career.

🎬 "IT'S A WRAP!"

Ellen Ripley's journey is more than a sci-fi story - it's a guidebook for leaders facing fear, chaos, and impossible odds. She teaches us that great leadership isn't about being fearless; it's about using fear as fuel. It's about standing up to systemic challenges, leading with empathy, and adapting to whatever the universe throws your way.

So, the next time you're staring down your own version of a Xenomorph—whether it's a tight deadline, a difficult colleague, or a seemingly impossible project—remember Ripley. Channel her courage, her resilience, and her unyielding sense of purpose. And when the time comes to step into the unknown, don't hesitate. Take a deep breath, look fear in the eye, and lead.

🎬 PRESENTED BY...

TANYA BOYD, PMP, PMI-ACP

Tanya Boyd is a dynamic project manager and creative strategist with 20+ years of experience across disaster recovery, healthcare, IT, marketing, and government.

As Director of Creative Collaboration at Corbeau and Project Success Academy, she blends imagination, strategy, and storytelling to spark bold programs, build partnerships, and design content that drives lasting success.

A PMP since 2014 and PMI-ACP since 2020, Tanya also led the PMI Baton Rouge Chapter as President, gaining a front-row seat to the evolving challenges of project leadership.

In 2024, she expanded into keynote speaking and educational video creation, producing a communication video series for Project Success Academy and the *From Risks to Rewards* course for PURE Management Alliance's 60-PDU credential.

She has delivered high-energy talks to 40+ PMI chapters and businesses on topics like generative AI, leadership, and workplace fears.

She believes curiosity and communication unlock creative solutions, with humor and storytelling as the secret sauce for unforgettable meetings. Off the clock, you'll find her kayaking Louisiana's swamps, camera in hand, chasing the next wild idea.

LINKEDIN
https://www.linkedin.com/in/tanya-boyd-pmp-project-personality/

PROJECT SUCCESS ACADEMY
https://projectsuccessacademy.com/

PURE MANAGEMENT ALLIANCE
https://www.puremanagementalliance.com#67586029bb967

TANYA BOYD PHOTOGRAPHY
https://www.tanyaboydphotography.com/

CHAPTER 13

IN THE LINE OF THE FIRES

Lava-Hot Lessons on Conflict and Crisis Leadership *(The Fires)*

The Fires (2025)
Logline: "Anna Arnardóttir, Iceland's top volcanologist, faces two disasters at once: a volcanic eruption that threatens the safety of the capital city and a love affair that could destroy her marriage."[14]

SETTING THE SCENE

THE FIRES IS AN ICELANDIC DRAMA ADAPTED FROM SIGRÍÐUR Hagalín Björnsdóttir's novel *The Fires: Love and Other Disasters*, written for the screen by Ugla Hauksdóttir and Markus Englmair. Set against the stark and volatile landscapes of Iceland's Reykjanes Peninsula, the film follows Anna Arnardóttir, a 42-year-old volcanologist at the University of Iceland, as she navigates a mounting geological crisis. Earthquakes begin to shake the region with increasing frequency and intensity, raising the specter of a major volcanic eruption after centuries of dormancy.

Anna is thrust into the public eye and into the heart of the Civil Protection Council's decision-making process. Her role demands she interpret incomplete scientific data, advise political leaders, and communicate with anxious communities—all while balancing competing agendas from government officials, the tourism industry, and fellow scientists. The professional challenges are compounded by personal strain: a tense marriage to Kristinn, a sense of guilt over time missed with her daughter Salka, and the growing emotional pull toward Thomas, a foreign photojournalist whose work captures both the raw force of the eruption and Anna's own moments of vulnerability.

The narrative blends the procedural urgency of disaster management with intimate explorations of human relationships. Anna's journey is as much about *(project)* leadership under pressure as it is about personal reckoning. The volcanic threat becomes a metaphor for her own internal turbulence—professional rivalries, political pressures, and private desires all shifting beneath the surface. Visually, the film contrasts the beauty and violence of Icelandic nature with the enclosed, tense spaces of coordination centers, town halls, and family homes. The drama invites reflection on the limits of scientific objectivity when filtered through human emotion, and how leaders respond when their credibility, ethics, and private lives are all on the line.

Anna's decisions reveal that absolute objectivity in project leadership is a myth; emotions, biases, and personal entanglements inevitably shape high-stakes calls. The challenge isn't eliminating them—it's leading through them.

> **HOT TAKE:** In The Fires, the most dangerous eruption isn't geological—it's inside the leader—the clash between personal vulnerability and the illusion of objectivity.

 THE MOVIE MOMENT

The room is tense when Anna Arnardóttir, a volcanologist and newly appointed representative on the restructured Natural Hazards Advisory Board, takes her seat opposite a small but powerful group: Ragnar from Civil Protection *(Iceland's police)*, Eiríkur from the Met Office, and two political and tourism stakeholders. This is not the scientific working group she's used to—this is politics in close quarters. The crisis at hand is the Kerlingarbás eruption, now apparently subsided. Seismic activity continues, but it is scattered and of lower magnitude. The question is: should the ***"Alert Phase"*** remain in effect, or is it time to scale back emergency measures?

Anna begins with caution. The data, though incomplete, suggests the ground is still restless. Earthquakes have shifted eastward toward the capital's volcanic systems. She explains that until the movement of magma can be confirmed or ruled out, the safest course is to maintain the heightened alert. Her tone is measured, but her underlying determination is clear—she is thinking not just of the science, but of the faces she saw in Grindavík when she reassured them weeks earlier. Faces that later looked back at her through ash and ruin.

The conversation pivots from hazard analysis to economic risk. The mood shifts when Sigríður María, representing tourism interests, warns of *"negative market impact."* The summer season is near, and tourists may hesitate to book trips under an active alert. Alternatively, she says, the eruption could make Iceland an even more popular destination for tourists eager to see a volcanic island and experience *"what it's like to live on the edge."*

Anna knows that putting tourists' safety at risk is not only morally unacceptable, but also could backfire and result in negative international press and an undesirable economic domino effect. Her patience thins. She reminds them, sharply, that their job is public safety, not crafting a palatable story for travelers. The clash is uncomfortable.

Ragnar, weighing both perspectives, opts to lift the Alert Phase, promising to reassess if clear evidence of imminent eruption emerges.

Anna sits back, unsettled. The decision feels premature, driven more by the need to calm markets than by geological reality. Later in the film, she points out that, *"The eruption can change its behavior without warning ... move to a new location. Rifts can open; the earth can literally swallow people."*

This moment distills the film's core tension: the collision between science and politics, between the objective need for caution and the subjective pressures of public perception and economic interest. It also exposes the human fault lines in Anna herself—her professional judgment colored by personal guilt, fatigue, and an intensifying need to be taken seriously in a male-dominated, politically charged space.

It's not just a meeting. It's a turning point where Anna as a leader must carry the weight of a choice she disagrees with, knowing that the earth, public trust—just like her own feelings and emotions—can shift without warning.

"ACTION!!!" PROJECTLAND SUCCESS TIPS

In Projectland, there can be entire projects that are born as a response to a crisis like the one illustrated by the movie moment above. Other projects have crisis moments and heated debates as leaders offer their own perspectives. Either way, project people are often under the microscope and need to make decisions quickly without the benefit of perfect information or a crystal ball that accurately predicts the future.

To help you navigate these heated situations, let´s introduce my new **F.I.R.E.S.** model! It is a tool for crisis project leaders to acknowledge the subjective influences on their judgment while maintaining as much objectivity as possible. Inspired by the Advisory Board scene in *The Fires*, it addresses the reality that in high-stakes environments, emotion, politics, and personal history inevitably shape decisions.

- **F - Frame the Facts First.** In moments of project crisis, it can be helpful to begin every discussion anchored in verified data before introducing opinions, scenarios, or hypotheticals. This approach ensures that all parties are grounded in a shared evidence base, limiting the space for distortion or selective interpretation.
- **I - Identify Emotional Drivers.** It is essential for project leaders to be conscious of their own internal pressures—whether guilt from past mistakes, conflict with colleagues, fatigue, or even personal relationships—that can color their judgment. Self-awareness enables you to differentiate between genuine risk signals and overcompensations that are born of deeper emotional needs and past experiences.
- **R - Respect Stakeholder Perspectives.** Even when political or economic agendas seem to oppose safety or other top priorities, it is essential to listen and understand the motivations behind them. Respectful engagement increases your credibility and influence, creating room for compromise..
- **E - Explore Scenarios.** By replacing rigid predictions with *"If–Then"* scenario framing and by outlining possible developments and associated responses, you can maintain flexibility, communicate uncertainty without causing panic, and keep stakeholders informed about the range of potential outcomes.
- **S - Sustain Composure Under Scrutiny.** In crisis leadership, how a message is delivered is as critical as its content. Maintaining a calm, professional tone—even when challenged or provoked—protects credibility and ensures the audience focuses on the substance rather than the emotion of the message.

The Advisory Board scene demonstrates that pure objectivity in crisis leadership is a myth. The real skill lies in recognizing subjective influences, managing them, and delivering decisions that balance top priorities, such as safety, politics, and public trust. The **F.I.R.E.S.** model equips leaders to do just that.

🎬 DIRECTOR'S COMMENTS

This scene from *The Fires* holds a special resonance for me, both professionally and personally. As a psychoanalyst, theologian, and crisis and conflict management consultant, I have spent decades studying how human beings make decisions under pressure. I know that objectivity is never as clean as we imagine—it is always colored by our fears, our desires, and the personal histories we carry into the room.

In the Advisory Board debate, Anna embodies that truth. She brings scientific expertise to the table, yet her words are shaped by guilt from earlier reassurances, the political tension of replacing a colleague, and the deep fatigue of living in constant crisis mode. I have seen this dynamic countless times in real-world emergencies—leaders wrestling with the collision between data and emotion. My connection to this scene is also deeply personal. I served as the safety officer during the shooting of *The Fires*, ensuring that our own *"crisis project"* ran safely amid unpredictable conditions. And, the other deeply personal twist is that the film's director, Ugla Hauksdóttir, is my daughter. Watching her bring to life this nuanced portrayal of leadership under pressure was both a professional fascination and a father's pride.

This movie moment captures what I love most about the film as whole: the raw honesty that leadership is not the absence of emotion, but the art of recognizing it—and still making the best possible call.

🎬 REALITY SHOW: WHEN LIFE IMITATES ART

One of the most striking truths in *The Fires* is how easily even the most seasoned professionals can slip from objectivity into the grip of their own subjectivity—while believing they are acting purely rationally. In the Advisory Board scene, Anna believes she is holding the scientific line, yet she is also carrying guilt, fatigue, rivalry, and emotional entanglement.

I have seen this countless times in my own version of Projectland—in crises where people's decisions are justified in the name of a *"method"* but are, in fact, deeply colored by emotion, bias, and psychological defense mechanisms. As a critically attuned academic and crisis and conflict management consultant, a highly trained mountaineering search and rescuer, and a frontline chaplain in emergency rooms, I have stood in the middle of storms—literal and figurative. I've dealt with blizzards, avalanches, raging stakeholders, violent project leaders, and emotionally volatile teams. In these moments, objectivity is often the first casualty. Feelings, cognitive biases, rationalizations, and justifications take over—individually and collectively—leading people astray.

Through years of facing chaos, I've learned that what works best is a *"warm heart"* and a *"cold mind."* This means maintaining an open, curious, and humane attitude, while keeping decision-making calm, analytical, and precise. It's a blend of empathy and detachment that allows you to lead without losing yourself to panic or ego. In my experience, when the going gets tough, the tough get playful—not reckless, but flexible and inventive in the face of pressure.

While writing this chapter, I invented the **F.I.R.E.S.** model to summarize what I have come across earlier in my work. Looking back, there were moments when I became overly entangled in the emotional currents of a team or organization, letting righteous indignation or the need to be *"right"* override my capacity to frame the facts clearly and explore scenarios openly.

With the **F.I.R.E.S.** model I could have more deliberately identified my own emotional drivers, respected opposing perspectives without absorbing their anxiety, and sustained composure while still advocating for safety and ethics.

One personal echo from *The Fires* makes this connection vivid. In the film, after a car accident, Anna runs towards a rescue team member—that's me, in a silent cameo, where I did my level best to harness my inner Clint Eastwood *"method acting"* style. Off-camera I've been that guy many times in real life—in the fog, in a whiteout, on the cliff, or in the middle of an organizational firestorm.

In those moments, the lesson is always the same: when chaos erupts, you need a heart that stays warm enough to connect with people, and a mind cold enough to navigate through the storm. That balance—between humanity and clarity—is what keeps you from becoming the next well-meaning leader who loses their objectivity in the name of objectivity itself.

🎞️ "IT'S A WRAP!"

We've journeyed from the volcanic tension of *The Fires*' Advisory Board scene to the real-world crucible of crisis leadership, exploring how even the most seasoned professionals can lose their grip on objectivity when emotions, biases, and personal histories flood the room.

Through Anna's story—and my own frontline experiences in crisis and conflict management, search and rescue, and emergency response—we've seen that pure rationality is a myth. The challenge is not to purge emotion, but to recognize it, manage it, and lead through it. The **F.I.R.E.S.** model—Frame the Facts, Identify Emotional Drivers, Respect Stakeholder Perspectives, Explore Scenarios, and Sustain Composure—was born from both cinematic and lived crisis moments. It offers a practical, repeatable way to keep a *"warm heart"* and a *"cold mind"* when everything around you is shaking, literally or figuratively.

My hope is that these star-studded success tips will serve as more than just leadership theory. The next time you're in your own version of Projectland—whether that's a boardroom battle, a community emergency, or a high-stakes negotiation—you'll remember that:

- Objectivity is strengthened, not weakened, by emotional self-awareness.
- Political, personal, and professional pressures will always exist; the key is how you navigate them.
- Leadership under pressure is less about controlling the storm and more about keeping your internal compass steady.

If Anna's fictional volcano taught us anything, it's that the ground can shift without warning. When it does, I want you to have the tools to stay grounded yourself, to lead decisively, and to walk out of the crisis knowing you kept both your integrity and your humanity intact. That, to me, is the real definition of success in project leadership.

🎬 PRESENTED BY...

DR HAUKUR INGI JÓNASSON

Dr Haukur Ingi Jónasson is a professor and the director of the Advanced Master of Project Management *(MPM)* program at Iceland's Reykjavik University. He holds a Cand. Theol. degree from the University of Iceland and a PhD in Psychiatry and Religion from Union Theological Seminary in New York. He received clinical training in pastoral counselling *(CPE)* at Lennox Hill Hospital / The HealthCare Chaplaincy Inc. and psychoanalytic training at the Harlem Family Institute.

A certified Stanford Project Manager, he is the co-author of multiple books on leadership, communication, project management, and strategy, including five titles published by Routledge/Taylor & Francis: *Project Ethics*; *Project: Leadership*; *Project: Communication*; *Project: Strategy*; and *Project: Execution*. He co-authored the International Project Management Association's *Code of Ethics and Professional Conduct* and is co-founder of Nordica Consulting Group ehf.

Beyond academia, Haukur is a mountaineer and member of the Reykjavik Air Ground Mountaineering Squad of the Icelandic Search and Rescue Association. His research interests span organizational behavior, conflict management, human development, coaching, and project ethics in diverse cultural settings.

Decades in crisis and conflict management, mountaineering rescues, and emergency response have shaped his philosophy: in the toughest moments, a leader must be able to be playful while keeping a ***"warm heart"*** and a ***"cold mind."*** For Haukur, the essence of leadership under pressure lies in mastering emotion, preserving clarity, and leading with both courage and humanity.

On a personal note, Haukur served as safety officer during the filming of ***The Fires*** and appeared briefly in a rescue scene. The film's director, Ugla Hauksdóttir, is his daughter, making the project a unique meeting of professional expertise and family pride.

CHAPTER 14

"LET'S WORK THE PROBLEM, PEOPLE"

How to Respond When Everything Seems Lost *(Apollo 13)*

Apollo 13
Log-line: "NASA must devise a strategy to return Apollo 13 to Earth safely after the spacecraft undergoes massive internal damage putting the lives of the three astronauts on board in jeopardy."[15]

SETTING THE SCENE

APOLLO 13 IS A FACT-BASED ACCOUNT OF NASA'S (AND HUmanity's) third manned mission to the moon. The Apollo program ran from 1961 to 1972. It was a series of missions aimed at landing humans on the Moon and safely returning them to Earth, and the first to achieve this goal (with Apollo 11) in 1969. The program conducted six successful Moon landings, advancing space exploration technology, and concluded with Apollo 17 as the last crewed lunar mission of the 20th century.

Apollo 13 was different. The craft left for the moon on April 11, 1970, carrying a crew of three: Jim Lovell (Tom Hanks) was Commander, with Fred Haise (Bill Paxton) slated to walk on the moon with him. Piloting the craft was Jack Swigert (Kevin Bacon). Swigert replaced the original pilot, Ken Mattingly (Gary Sinese), after a health scare. Meanwhile, mission control monitored everything from Houston, Texas.

Two days into the flight, NASA control instructed the crew to carry out a routine operation that triggered a short circuit, a fire, and a catastrophic explosion. As alarms sounded and lights flashed, Lovell calmly sent the message everyone feared: *"Houston, we have a problem."*

The service module, which provided power and services to the command module that the three astronauts were living in, had become near useless after the explosion. The only thing that was undamaged was the Lunar Excursion Module (LEM). This was the small (two-person) craft designed to land on the moon, support two astronauts for a few days, and return to the command module. It was this craft that became the lifeboat that would get the astronauts back to Earth.

However, the LEM could never enter the Earth's atmosphere. For that, they would need to return to the command module with its three seats, heat shield, and parachutes.

They needed to answer some important questions to survive. If they made it back to Earth's orbit in the LEM, could they power up the command module to finish the journey into Earth's atmosphere? Was the heat shield still intact? And would the parachutes deploy and return the three men back to Earth safely?

From the very start of this film, we are aware that what NASA and its astronauts are trying to achieve is audacious and dangerous. At the heart of their ability to succeed are four things. And this film illustrates them clearly.

It does so in two ways. First, in the way the astronauts, engineers, and support teams conduct themselves while events are still routine. I use this word 'routine' cautiously; getting to the moon may never be routine, and certainly was not in 1970. Second, when circumstances became extraordinary, the film shows the essential lessons for what allowed the NASA of the late 1960s and early 1970s to be so successful.

> **HOT TAKE:** Projects don't need heroes. They need professionals who work together, unrelentingly; falling back on rigor, professionalism, and discipline.

 THE MOVIE MOMENT

The big movie moment comes when the three astronauts in the LEM learn they're running out of breathable air. Every breath they take exchanges life-giving oxygen for toxic carbon dioxide (CO_2). Onboard both the command module and the LEM were scrubbers. A scrubber is a device that removes excess CO_2 from the air, to maintain a breathable atmosphere. Unfortunately, the LEM only has enough scrubbers to support the two astronauts it was designed for. With three men in the LEM, they were being poisoned by their own breathing!

Fortunately, the command module also has scrubbers. But using them in the LEM was not a contingency that the design teams had anticipated. And because the two crafts were built by different contractors, the scrubber units aren't compatible; the command module scrubbers are square, but the LEM scrubbers (and the ports that accepted them) are round.

NASA must very quickly find a way to fit a square peg into a round hole.

"ACTION!!!" PROJECTLAND SUCCESS TIPS

The movie's characters had to solve a fiendishly complicated problem, with severely limited resources, against a tight deadline, and where the outcome was life or death. This is exactly what happened in real life, so the lessons we learn from the movie are genuine.

Their success began with an orientation towards the future; by asking, "What *can* we do?" The alternative is an orientation towards the past, which asks, "What happened to get us here?" and encourages a search for blame. This has no use in the present moment when you must find a solution. Sometimes, understanding how things happened can feed into problem solving. But mostly, we should save that kind of thinking for after we have fixed the problem and, in this case, brought the astronauts home safely.

The next lesson is also critical. What we see on screen is an absolute determination to succeed. No one tore at their hair and said, "Dammit! This can't be done!" Instead, we see engineers sleeping in offices, fueled by coffee and grit, getting on with the job.

This comes from character, culture, and leadership. These are three of the four lessons I drew from the film, as a whole. This means that, as a project leader, you need to hire for character, build a culture, and lead with compassion, commitment, and rigor.

But the success tips I want to draw from 'the scrubbers' sequence is supremely practical. It is the deliberate process that we saw the engineers use in the film. The sequence begins with a wonderfully simple brief: "Well, I suggest you gentlemen invent a way to put a square peg in a round hole."

What is particularly important about this (beyond its courtesy and brevity) is that it states the problem in the form of the solution they need to find. It's not "The square scrubber won't go into the round hole", which merely states what's wrong.

From there, we see a deliberate problem-solving process. It started with a short motivational message: "The people upstairs have handed us this one, and we've got to come through." Everyone knew why. Clarity of the mission and the brief are the right way to start problem-solving. We then see five steps.

- **Discuss**: They clarify what they need to achieve and immediately move towards.
- **Inventory resources**: The team on the ground assembles every resource available to the astronauts and nothing else. *"Right, let's get it organized,"* the team leader says. This is always time well spent. Understand what you have and make it easy to access.
- **Step by step**: What we don't see is the process of trial and error and aha moments that led to a solution. But we know about it from another parallel sub-plot in the film. In that story line, astronaut Ken Mattingly relentlessly tried everything he could to solve the problem of crafting a power-up sequence that did not demand more current than the system had available. We know the team tried everything and anything.
- **Document the process**: With a solution in hand, the team then takes the time to document the process. They create a checklist. This is critical in the aeronautics sector yet under-appreciated by many project professionals. With a single step-by-step sequence of actions spelled out clearly and precisely, the Houston team found and then secured a solution. With a precise checklist, it could be implemented swiftly in space.
- **Communicate clearly**: There is one more step that matters. No solution is any good if the people on the ground (or in space) cannot implement it correctly. This requires good communication. Beyond the careful documentation, we see the important role of Capcom (Capsule Communications). This is a single point of communication with the men in space. And Capcom was always someone who speaks the same way the astronauts do; one of their peers.

MAKE A DECISION

One final, critical point to make here. Between finding the solution and implementing it is an important moment: a decision. In this scenario, we see the Flight Director, Gene Kranz (Ed Harris), as a single point of authority. In a crisis situation, this is especially important.

FOUR KEYS TO SUCCESS

If you want a checklist for what it takes to succeed at an extraordinary endeavor, this film gives it to you. Here we see clearly the impact of:

- **Culture**: A culture that balances concern for safety with a willingness to take risks, and one that values science and engineering equally alongside the lives and needs of the astronauts.
- **Attitude**: From the astronauts to the junior engineers, there is an extraordinary optimism that is justified by a commitment to science, data, and evidence, alongside a can-do belief that anything is possible with enough commitment and understanding.
- **Leadership**: Throughout the film, we see exceptional examples of leadership, from the calm competence of mission commander, Jim Lovell, and the steady determination of flight director, Gene Kranz, to Apollo 11 commander Neil Armstrong's quiet willingness to sit with Lovell's aged mother.
- **Process**: Leadership is not just about vision and inspiration. It sits alongside a solid understanding of the importance of process in delivering predictable results. It is as much this rational and meticulous approach as the leadership and attitude that returned the Apollo crew safely to Earth.

This quote from Gene Kranz captures all four of these elements: "Let's work the problem people. Let's not make things worse by guessing."

DIRECTOR'S COMMENTS

I love this movie because the Apollo program was a tremendous demonstration of the potential of humankind. And the response to the crisis of Apollo 13 showed our spirit at its best.

This is a movie moment where we get to cheer a small triumph by the normally unseen experts who work tirelessly to invent, make, mend, and reimagine things, day in and day out. And yet it is also a moment that reminds us that solving one problem, no matter how great an achievement, is often just one step towards solving a bigger, more complex, and more consequential problem. The striving never stops.

I've encountered plenty of problems on projects, but nothing like this—thankfully. But my favorite recollection was a team leader telling me that he thought his team had *"f****d up."* They were on a deadline and the numbers did not add up. And no one could see why.

This is a job for a project manager. And it's the reason why we shouldn't take on too much during the delivery phase of a project. We need to be free to see the big picture, be available to our teams, and be able to roll our sleeves up and lead the team to find a solution.

But, for me, finding a solution was *not* about solving the math. That's not what a project manager does. It was about finding the resources and the people to solve the problem quickly. I made a couple of calls and secured a forensic accountant who dropped everything to get in a cab and join the team.

The right team to solve a problem has people with a range of relevant skills, the trust to listen to each other and test ideas, and a focus on the details that matter.

What really inspired me in Apollo 13's problem-solving sequence were the rational-scientific mindsets of a team of engineers that knew they had to come through.

And, come through they did.

For their effort, the person who represented the team got the ultimate appreciation anyone could show in that culture. "You, sir, are a steely-eyed missile man," said Capcom, once the astronauts had fitted a square peg in a round hole. Leaders must always celebrate the success of their teams and recognize the efforts they make.

🎥 REALITY SHOW: WHEN LIFE IMITATES ART

A key role of a project manager is to get the right team together to resolve the problem at hand. This is mirrored in Honda's operational practice of *Waigaya*. This draws together a babble of problem solvers to discuss and curate a solution to a problem. Everyone is equal and every idea belongs to the team, not to the person who makes the suggestion. Keys to this method's success include that the solution needs to be one everyone can own, and it must be one that can be implemented. Often, this means documenting it clearly.

Early in my career, I was tasked with facilitating a negotiation among four parties to a complex commercial agreement in the UK rail industry. Some of the choices I made seem, on reflection, to have been influenced by the way the team worked together and documented their findings in this sequence.

To start, I sat everyone around a round table. That was a deliberate choice because there are no sides. This was the best shot I had at creating an atmosphere of collaboration from the start.

I also spent a lot of time breaking the problem into each constituent conversation we needed to have, and sequencing them logically. I then produced a decision sheet that listed every topic on which we needed to document an agreed position. Under each heading was space to record the consensus.

I wanted to be certain that everyone had exactly the same text on their sheets. So, I printed my own copy at the size of flip chart paper. After each conversation, I would make a trial close (a technique for collecting validation feedback through open-ended questions). I would read out, from my notes, what I thought the position was. We might tweak that, but once we had an agreed statement, I wrote it on the flip chart form and suggested everyone copy my text onto their worksheet, verbatim. This was, by the way, in the mid 1990s. Now, of course, we'd all whip out our phones and take a photo.

Having a solid process and a clear articulation of the solution meant that, by the end, we had a shared document that I could pass to the lawyers to incorporate into the contract terms. And we were certain that we collectively owned the solution.

🎬 "IT'S A WRAP!"

Next time you find yourself with a problem to solve, I do hope it is not life or death! But whatever it is, you will have the best chance of solving it when the culture is right, you have people with a positive, can-do attitude, led by a pragmatic leader, and you follow a solid process.

There is another chapter in this book inspired by a different movie that sets advanced problem-solving in space: *The Martian*. It's a wonderful film, and I love it, and the chapter brilliantly applies the lessons to adaptive problem-solving. Fortunately, project professionals on Earth do not work alone. We have the luxury to draw on a team to support us and our projects. And that means that our skills need to be less about solving problems and "sciencing the shit out of them," and focus on leading teams and inspiring excellence from them. Our job is to bring the right people together so they can "science the shit out of" the problems we face. In either case, adaptiveness and perseverance are key.

🎬 PRESENTED BY...

DR. MIKE CLAYTON

Dr. Mike Clayton is a physicist, a project manager, an educator, and a communicator. He's written 15 print books (for 6 international publishers) and runs OnlinePMCourses.com, which offers free and paid training, knowledge, and resources for project professionals. His YouTube channel, @OnlinePMCourses, is the second largest Project Management channel, with over 600 videos on all aspects of the discipline.

Mike is available to speak at business and project management events, large and small.

CHAPTER 15

SMOKE OUT 'DEM DEADLY SNAKES

Building Trust & Sidestepping Sabotage *(The Italian Job)*

The Italian Job (2003)
Logline: "After being betrayed and left for dead in Italy, Charlie Croker and his team plan an elaborate gold heist against their former ally."[16]

SETTING THE SCENE

IF YOU READ MY BOOK, *MEET THE PLAYERS IN PROJECTLAND: Decide the Right Project Roles & Get People on Board*, then you know that most projects fail, people are typically the root cause, and there is a player in Projectland who is known as the saboteur. This stakeholder, who is outside the project team, is represented by the snake. There is also a story about Stakeholder Gabby, a cheerleader for a project, who accidentally became a saboteur.

But what if the snake is embedded on your team? That's exactly what happens in *The Italian Job*. Like all good heist movies, unforeseen circumstances arise that could sabotage their success, and the crew has to deal with them under severe time pressure. I think every project I've ever dealt with has been under severe time pressure. After all, no project sponsor worth their salt says, *"Take all the time you need,"* and means it.

Two lines woven throughout the movie serve as great lessons for Projectland. One is a lesson imparted by Donald Sutherland's character and later repeated by others: When someone is asked how they are and replies that they're *"fine,"* what FINE really means is:

Freaked out

Insecure

Neurotic, and

Emotional

The second axiom offered by the same character is, *"Trust everyone. Just don't trust the devil inside them."*

The truth is that people can make or break your projects, and this movie illustrates that in spades. Whether it's an actual saboteur on your team, circumstances that stress us out, insecurities we have, or a risk we didn't see coming, do not expect everything to go smoothly. It won't.

> **HOT TAKE:** In Projectland, watch out for who and what could sabotage your success, have your head on a swivel, and be ready to deal with whatever obstacles come your way.

🍿 THE MOVIE MOMENT

As the movie begins, a crew of thieves, led by master safecracker John Bridger *(Donald Sutherland)* and his protégé and mastermind Charlie Croker *(Mark Wahlberg)*, steal a safe full of gold in Venice. Every successful project should end with a celebration, and this one does too. When the crew is safely in the snowy mountains with their ill-gotten gold, they're standing in a circle outside drinking champagne. One by one they share what they'd like to do with their share of the loot. *"Handsome Rob"* (*Jason Statham*) wants an Aston Martin Vanquish. Lyle, the team's tech genius *(Seth Green)* has his heart set on a NAD T770 digital decoder with 70-watt amps and Burr-Brown DACs. They tell him to speak English. He explains that it's a big stereo with speakers *"so loud that they blow women's clothes off."* With that explanation, they all agreed that his stereo was a great idea. *"Left Ear,"* the crew's demolition expert *(Yasiin Bey, otherwise known as Mos Def)* says he wants a villa in the south of Spain with a room for his shoes. When the question comes around to Steve *(Ed Norton)* he looks around and shrugs and says, *"I liked what you said. I'll take one of each of yours."*

Soon after this, they're on the road again and begin to cross a bridge. Another vehicle is coming straight at them and then stops to block their way. Steve turns a gun on Handsome Rob, who's driving. When Rob frantically asks what he's doing, Steve says, *"I made some plans of my own."* He double-crosses them, kills the patriarch safecracker of the group, and leaves the rest of them for dead.

Meanwhile back in Philadelphia, Stella Bridger *(Charlize Theron)*, is cracking safes like her father, except legitimately and for the police. When Charlie walks into her business and asks for her help in stealing the gold back from Steve, she initially declines. Later she changes her mind and most of the guys aren't sure she's up for the task. She's no career criminal and as Handsome Rob warns, *"there are no guarantees in this business."* The foreshadowing was excellent, because later her preference to use technology to help her crack Steve's safe fails her, and she must do it by touch like her dad.

"ACTION!!!" PROJECTLAND SUCCESS TIPS

I love a good heist movie, and part of the reason is because the people, the plan, and the team's ability to navigate things that don't go according to plan runs absolutely parallel to every major project in my career, minus the murder.

> *"Planning is important, but the most important part of every plan is to plan on the plan not going according to plan."*
>
> — Morgan Housel, author of The Psychology of Money[17]

Why do things not go according to plan? Sometimes it's because you're in unknown territory. After all, the definition of a project includes that it's unique, so you couldn't possibly know everything there is to know about the journey, the bumps, and the creatures you might face there. Welcome to Projectland! Other times, it's because the people are unprepared, have their own agendas, or can't stand the pressure cooker experience that a high-profile, high-pressure, visible project brings. In *The Italian Job*, all of these hiccups happen.

If the team could have figured out that Steve was a snake amongst them before it was too late, and before he killed their friend and stole the gold for himself, they could have avoided the whole mess. It's not always possible, but when project leaders invest even a small amount of effort into stakeholder identification and analysis, they are often surprised and relieved by the result. It's best to know who the snake is, where they are, and consider their motivation so you can plan to do something about it.

To illustrate the importance of getting to know your teammates, I really enjoyed how the players on the heist team get introduced in the movie, too. After Stella agrees to help, Charlie explains how each of the team members got their start, and the scenes flash back to their childhoods *(where, incidentally, the child actors look so much like the adults!)*. Even Shawn Fanning, the founder of Napster, makes an appearance as himself, and later Lyle insists on being called ***"The Napster,"*** claiming that Shawn was his college roommate who stole his idea while he was napping. Each of us might have hangups from our past that can creep up on us and impact our performance.

To gel as a strong team, it's helpful for us to get to know each other as humans. What makes us tick? There's always something that makes us unique and can help or hurt our ability to be great team members. Learning the backgrounds of the characters did certainly help me to understand them as I watched the movie. Interestingly enough, we don't know how Steve got his start. If we did, perhaps it would have helped us be more wary of him as a trusted team member.

📣 DIRECTOR'S COMMENTS

I had to learn about saboteurs in Projectland the hard way. Since my biological mother left my father and me when I was about two years old, I have had plenty of trust issues to face over the years. But I tended to take people at face value at work for some reason. I always want to make my own assessment of who people are without having others' opinions taint how I see them. I will listen, but I form my own opinion. Probably since I was insecure and bullied as a kid, I want to do the opposite of what I experienced and give everyone a fair shot. However, now I know that stressful situations tend to amplify people's dark sides, and Projectland is definitely stressful. This is where the FINE and the ***"don't trust the devil inside them"*** lessons come in handy.

The other part of the movie that really hit me was when Stella was introduced to the team, and most of the guys weren't sure she was up for the job. She was the only woman on the team, and when I joined a tech consulting firm back in the late 90's, I started as the only woman in the cohort of new hires. Countless times in my career, I was the only woman on the team or in the room.

🎬 REALITY SHOW: WHEN LIFE IMITATES ART

Grrr… Snakes! Here's one example from when I was working as a project manager onsite with a client and discovered a sneaky snake saboteur. There was a steering team member who I later realized killed a project because he wanted the new female leader to fail, and because if her project succeeded, him not doing his job well for the past decade would be exposed. No one saw that one coming as he was a highly respected leader who had quite a bit of tenure there.

You just really never know people, and if they have a nefarious agenda, they are probably not going to tell you. However, if you get a feeling that something is off, like I did when I first heard Steve say he'll take what everyone else wants, definitely listen to that intuition! Every single time I didn't listen to my intuition in Projectland, I regretted it.

It's tough to be the new kid on the block. At first, I didn't even notice that Stella was the sole woman on the team, just like I often didn't notice when it happened to me. Perhaps her gender didn't matter to the team members either. They needed an expert safecracker, but was she the right fit for the role? They were worried she was too emotional since Steve killed her dad, and Charlie defended her by reminding them that they were all emotional about this one, since, after all, her dad was their friend.

I consider myself fortunate to have been on strong teams with all men, and there were many times where a few of them weren't so sure about me at first. No one is ever sure about the new person, especially if they'd already formed a solid team. It was just like being the nervous new kid at school all over again. Generally, I found the situation to be quite understandable and took no offense. After all, when you look at the classic stages of the teaming process *(forming, storming, norming, performing, adjourning/mourning)*, adding a new person starts the whole teaming process at forming again, which is challenging for everyone.

When Charlie came to Stella's defense, I had flashbacks from the many times a man who was respected by the team stepped up and vouched for me. Many of these moments have added up over the years and have meant all the difference in my career. Every time this happened, it opened a door for me to prove myself. Stella, too, gets the chance to prove herself, and her gender even becomes an asset. By stepping up and doing what needed to be done to help the team, she earns the respect of the guys. In fact, there was a turning point when I felt the shift in her being accepted as a full-fledged team member well before she was faced with cracking a safe.

🎬 "IT'S A WRAP!"

Here are three quick summary lessons that I hope will help you tackle your version of Projectland.

There's almost always a snake around somewhere. If you don't know who the snake is, you better figure it out before you're happily skipping through a meadow in Projectland toward your goal and it jumps up and bites you in the ankle when you least expect it. Who might hate your project? Who might want the project to fail? Who might feel threatened, annoyed, or negative about the project? These are your potential snakes, and you need to create a plan to manage them before they wreak havoc on your project or even get it killed.

Teaming is a Process. While there are snakes to be wary of, you also need to be able to trust your teammates. Like Charlie did for Stella, when you can give someone a chance who you feel can do the job, do what you need to do to help skeptical team members give them a fair shot. And if you're the newbie team member like Stella, do your best to prove that they were right in choosing you by demonstrating that you're a valuable part of the team. If you're the seasoned pro who's skeptical about the newbie, remember that if they fail, so do you. You're all in this together. Instead, keep an open mind and actively help them integrate into the team, so you can all climb your way back up to *"performing"* quickly. Otherwise, you are potentially a saboteur.

Risks and Issues are Part of Projectland. Just like there are no guarantees in the business of thievery, there are no guarantees in Projectland either. While it's best to plan for risks ahead of time, you can't plan for them all. Like Stella discovered when the safe she had to crack was not the Worthington 1000 model she expected, you too will run into unexpected surprises that'll test your mettle. You don't know what they'll be, but it helps to be aware that there'll very likely be obstacles to overcome. Fortunately, when Stella doubted herself, Charlie expressed his belief in her, which helped her keep going. Teamwork really can make the dream work, particularly when the going gets tough.

If you'd like to dive deeper and get related practical tips, there are two whole chapters in *Meet the Players in Projectland* that cover these concepts: Chapter 11 – *What to Do About Stakeholders, Especially the Difficult Ones* and Chapter 12 - *Get Ready For The Storm: Teaming Is a Process, Too.*

 **PRESENTED BY...**

DAWN MAHAN, PMP

Dawn Mahan is the founder of PMOtraining, LLC and author of the Amazon #1 Bestseller, *Meet the Players in Projectland: Decide the Right Project Roles & Get People On Board*.

She is a dynamic international speaker, a Project Management Institute *(PMI)* certified leader with extensive global experience, and sole inventor of the *ProjectFlo® Process Learning System* that makes learning PMI's complex process fast, easy, and fun. She works with C-level leaders, business owners in growth mode, PMO leaders, and project managers at all levels. Her work in preparing young professionals in the YearUp program for internships at major companies has been featured in Morningstar, Yahoo! Finance and more.

In 2009, she left the Fortune 50 and started her own firm. In 2014, she was awarded Professional of the Year Consulting/Project Management by Strathmore Who's Who Worldwide. In 2021, she was hired by Udemy as their project management expert to co-create *Smart Tips: Project Management & Agile* for their business and marketplace platforms. She has trained thousands of ambitious professionals around the world.

Dawn has built houses in Cambodia with Habitat for Humanity, has played a variety of roles on the American Lung Association's Philadelphia Leadership Board, and sponsors a girls' flag football team in Florida.

When she's not in Projectland, you can most often find her with family in Hawaii, Pennsylvania, or the Florida Keys.

CHAPTER 16

NAVIGATING EGOS & CULTURES

A Wild Ride from the Saddle of Vendor Delivery *(The Man from Snowy River)*

The Man from Snowy River
Logline: "In 1880s Australia, after young Jim Craig's father dies, he takes a job at the Harrison cattle ranch, where he is forced to become a man."[18]

SETTING THE SCENE

THE MAN FROM SNOWY RIVER WAS INSPIRED BY A POEM. IN the Australian high country of the Snowy Mountains and the low country on the plains, the 1880s was the gold rush era.

Our movie begins before the title rolls, with whistling winds and a bleak landscape. From the thunderous sound of wild horses galloping across the screen, the scene shifts to the warmth of the mountain home of young Jim Craig *(Tom Burlinson)* and his father as they discuss their financial woes. When a herd of wild horses run by, they see an opportunity to capture and sell some of them.

Sadly, Jim's father is killed in the mayhem of the stampede. Now, Jim must find a way to make it on his own. One of the mountain men sternly tells him, **"Look, you go down to the low country and earn the right to live up here, just like your father did."** But the mountains and the plains are two different worlds—and so it's a harsh reality check: Jim must go to a strange land and make money.

Down in the low country, Jim finds himself working for Harrison *(Kirk Douglas)*. Here, Jim is the outsider because he comes from the high country—seemingly resented by others, though he doesn't understand why.

Egos run rampant. On one side there are risk-takers and on the other there are rule makers, each with completely different perspectives. Naturally, buttons get pressed and rash assumptions are made.

This is a coming-of-age story of Jim and Jessica *(Sigrid Thornton)* as they learn about themselves and about navigating the world around them. It's also about people dynamics, and how a kind, experienced, and respected mentor can make all the difference in navigating tough terrain, opposing cultures, and mighty egos.

> **HOT TAKE:** The right mentor can make all the difference in navigating tough terrain, opposing cultures, and mighty egos.

 THE MOVIE MOMENT

Let's take a look inside some of the people dynamics in *The Man from Snowy River*, starting with the scene where Clancy, a mentor, is about to make his entrance.

Frew becomes animated and explains, **"Clancy is not just a horseman. Clancy's a magician. He's a genius."**

Jim says, **"I've met him ... when I was young. He and my father were mates."** But the men, including Frew and a particularly antagonistic character, Curly, laugh and brush him off—dismissing the idea that this naïve kid could know Clancy.

All the men gather to see Clancy arrive. He must be someone important. Curly's disdain of Jim is written on his face.

When Clancy greets Jim and validates that his father was his friend, Frew changes his tune. He nods his respect at Jim, and Jim gains a new ally. In that moment of acknowledgement, Jim is elevated and given respect. Well, apart from Curly.

During the movie, Clancy, who has arrived from the mountains to join in the rounding up of the beef cattle herd that are across the mountain, subtly discovers the points of view of people around him and kindly gets his own points across. He seems to have no ego and he's not keeping score. Instead, there is an eloquence of composure, despite his clearly respected position.

Clancy is the guest of honor at dinner that evening with Harrison, Banjo Paterson, Jessica *(Harrison's daughter)*, and Mrs. Rosemary Hume. Clancy is happy in both worlds: the mountains and the plains.

This evening, Harrison's ego is on full display with his verbose stories about what he has achieved. As long as the diners flatter his ego, all is well. The tide turns when Clancy and Mrs. Hume share their views.

Jim knocks on the door and brings more firewood into the room.

Clancy says to Jim, *"Mr. Harrison was just talking of taming the Snowy River country. You know it better than any of us. What do you think?"*

Jim innocently answers, *"Well, sir, I think you might sooner hold back the tide, than tame the mountains."*

Jim leaves. Banjo and Clancy seem impressed, while Harrison makes a snide remark about the mountain people.

Clancy asks if that sentiment includes Harrison's brother, Spur. At this point, Harrison says, *"I have no brother."* He has had enough and strides out of the room.

Soon we learn that Harrison decided to no longer include Jim in the cattle muster. He is quick to retaliate when things do not go his way.

"ACTION!!!" PROJECTLAND SUCCESS TIPS

I am usually a crime buff, yet I found this movie fascinating. It has these nuances of egos, angst, and moods that change like the weather. It feels like one of those challenging projects where you just know you're in for a wild ride. Even though you're confident that you know how to deliver, you can see that the people management side is going to take time and test your emotional intelligence. I've found this situation to be particularly true as a consultant leading Software as a Service *(SaaS)* implementation projects.

If you've been through a major SaaS implementation, perhaps you're groaning as you recall the saddle sores you earned from the bumpy ride. Perhaps you were the client and your team wasn't ready to start, and yet your SaaS provider's project manager was already out of the gate and taking the reins. This is when client project leaders are often thinking, *"Hey, this is my project,"* or *"Wait, are we talking a different language?"* In many cases, client managers assign folks to *"just do this little piece of work, alongside your day job,"* but they are not fully briefed and SaaS projects aren't their expertise.

Just like the film's writers must have struggled with transforming a poem into a movie, and Jim struggled to navigate two different worlds, vendor SaaS providers and their customers who are new to implementing the SaaS solution, often have two very different cultures that collide.

If everyone is doing their own thing, the job is not getting done. The vendor and customer teams need to work together as one cohesive unit working toward the same goal.

If you're new to this situation and assigned to lead it, having a calm, experienced mentor while you earn your spurs, can help you to navigate the people dynamics and opposing cultures. This can result in a positive difference in the tone of the delivery and your ability to navigate inevitable nuances.

Clancy is that mentor for Jim. In the movie, Jim and his mountain horse navigate what feels akin to the fast pace of project delivery. And like Jim experienced, there are glances and subtle expressions to note as relationships ebb and flow and you learn what is possible. During the project it may not always feel rosy and people are often not direct about how they feel.

Even if no such mentor exists in your organization, there are tips to help smooth the way.

> *"If ego is the voice that tells us we're better than we really are, we can say ego inhibits true success by preventing a direct and honest connection to the world around us."*
>
> — Ryan Holiday, author of Ego is the Enemy[19]

A project is a deliverable, the SaaS is the tangible asset, and yet the customer and their project team are not always dedicated 100% to the project because they have day jobs. As the consultant project manager who has performed many similar implementations, I can share a Gantt chart, risk registers, and all the standard project assets. But the technique that most often makes a difference is lifting my head above the weeds and seeing that we are in Projectland—with all the ***"people nuances"*** that go with it.

No matter how well I know the SaaS product and the steps to deliver, it is critical to remember that the customer is brand new to this world. With any transformation project, the people are both the key to success and the challenge. Some people will be your allies. And some may start as your ally and then switch, trying to take control or get the upper hand.

I've learned that I don't always have the right insights about the culture and people up front. So it's best to build relationships quickly, while you navigate the terrain. The more you know about people, the easier it is to lead them through the steep mountains, rivers, and creeks, or on the wild ride down the mountainside toward the goal.

In the movie, Harrison takes tight control and acts a lot like a customer sponsor who attempts to also perform the project manager role. When this happens, they are their own saboteur, pushing away those who want to be project cheerleaders. As a vendor partner, I am always looking for ways to enable customers—even the ones like Harrison who have giant egos—and help them maintain their image. This is not always possible.

I like the way that Jim, Clancy, and Spur work as a team to lighten the load for each other. It isn't about who is doing better than the other. It is about calling out when team members have stepped back when they need to step up—and they may not have even realized it. The actors demonstrate well that cohesion with your project team is key when there are challenges. Being able to flex and work as a team eases the pressure for any one individual.

Harrison's controlling nature pushes people away and creates an environment and culture that allows Curly to act like a sabotaging snake. Harrison is hurting himself and his chances of success without realizing it. Unfortunately, I've seen this happen many times in Projectland.

Personality clashes can lead to delayed or cancelled projects, where the cost to both the vendor and customer is immense. For instance, the lost investment in time and money, the impact on customers and their benefits realizations which are linked to their Objectives and Key Results *(OKRs)*, or reduction in the vendor's forecasted Monthly Recurring Revenue *(MRR)*.

Once delivery is finally achieved, there should be some healthy reflection. Relationships often shift when the project team, both the vendor and customer, comes together to celebrate and reflect on their lessons learned.

Over the years, I've learned that especially on projects where two cultures need to come together to form a team and deliver rapidly, it's best to begin to build relationships before the kickoff and understand the terrain. On SaaS projects, this means that the client sponsor, client project manager, and vendor project manager need to take the time to align. I've also learned that big egos can kill projects, so the earlier you can identify this risk, the quicker you can strategize to navigate around it. For instance, finding, assigning, or being a calm mentor like Clancy to guide and support project leaders in navigating the terrain can make all the difference.

📣 DIRECTOR'S COMMENTS

This movie was introduced to me by my grandfather. We watched it together when it came on the TV in the UK each year. It was our mutual love of horses that drew me to the film, not the coming-of-age story, the big egos, or even the love story. I noticed each of these elements as I grew into an adult. I even started to see the family dynamics in the film showing up in my own family. It helped me to discover my role as listener and supporter.

By watching this movie every year—with the thunderous hooves, the wind, the music that goes with the horses, the feeling of being up on the bluff with the snow, and that moment Jim and his horse gallop down the mountainside and my grandfather and I held our breath together—I realized I love to take risks. It might have taken me a few years, but that realization, thanks to this film, led me to become a circumnavigator on the Clipper Round the World Yacht Race.

This movie shows us both the big picture of life and its intricacies. I like both, which is another reason that I'm drawn to this movie. I love to navigate the tricky terrain of cultures, people, and projects. While I sit in the UK most of the time, I am thrilled to work with people worldwide. No matter the situation, for me egos are best left at the door. It's no wonder that Ryan Holiday wrote an entire book called *Ego is the Enemy*.

🎥 REALITY SHOW: WHEN LIFE IMITATES ART

GRRR... IS IT A LION, TIGER, LIGER OR TIGON?

On a SaaS project where I was the senior leader representative for the software vendor, I came across a hybrid client creature quite like Harrison. If you read *Meet the Players in Projectland: Decide the Right Project Roles & Get People on Board*, then you know that the animal avatar for the sponsor is the lion, the king *(or queen!)* of the jungle. And the animal avatar for the project manager is the tiger—not the biggest cat in town, but awfully close. Both Harrison and this client decided that they should be both. Were they a liger? A tigon? I wasn't sure, but I knew their very declaration of taking on both roles wasn't a good start to the engagement. These roles are separate and distinct on purpose!

First, the client sponsor decided that our vendor project manager was not good enough and proceeded to tell me how a project should be run and why they would not work with our project manager. They declared that the project manager was not senior enough and would require my presence to take them through the project. Next, they wanted to make sure I knew the Project Management Institute's standards. Then, they tried to use their job title and the size of the company to undermine and control us, attempting to not only steer who was on the project team, but also to delay the project whenever they wanted at no cost. Our project manager liked the challenge but needed someone with a title to push back respectfully. That was my role in the first instance, to mentor the project manager. Plus, the first line of escalation fell to me as the Director, before we moved up to a C-Suite level leader. These situations can be tough and time is critical.

My first action in these situations is to listen to both sides separately, as this is absolutely key to knowing where I am negotiating from.

VENDOR PROJECT MANAGER

- Provide an honest account as they see the situation
- Open honest discussion
- Presents and discusses the possible options
- Change of project team member(s), including themselves, the project manager
- Contractual – calculate the delay costs
- Recompense – yes, we do consider this as a last resort

CLIENT

- Meet face to face or via online meeting
- Ask the client what they would like to happen
- Clients will often come to the table with their demands
  - Project team changes
  - Delaying the project
  - $'s they are prepared to accept

Then we have our basis of where I can begin to negotiate. Before I negotiate, I will always thank them for their candor, as we are starting from a foundation of open communication. On this project the project manager stayed in place, we delayed the project go-live for three months, and it was agreed that I would attend the next three project meetings to support the project manager, ensuring that agendas and risks are managed.

I was thankful that I previously had experienced a similar situation. On my first experience, I didn't understand the dynamic and the game play. I was left with a cancelled project and fortunately negotiated a clean exit. However, it's never good when you have to back out of the deal and lose the forecasted revenue. Back then, I hadn't realized the nuance of making this type of client creature look good. It was a harsh lesson to learn. Now I'm always on the lookout for big egos and ask the team to share when something feels off. These animals don't often show all their true colors up front or at the same time.

I was encouraged and grateful that our project manager was like Jessica, in a dramatic scene later in the film, where she is on a ledge and cries out for help. Other project managers might ask to be reassigned immediately or carry on without saying anything while burning out under the pressure. My view is that we are a team, and I was happy to lean on my previous real-world experience to help navigate the culture, tone, and those lovely egos—mine included.

"IT'S A WRAP!"

Here are three quick summary lessons that I hope will help you tackle your version of Projectland.

Identify the egos. Do you know who your potential saboteur leaders are? One way to spot them is to notice who likes their title and seeks recognition for themselves before everyone else. Watch how leaders control the room and conversations. Observe if the mood darkens quickly when they arrive or if the team insists that all decisions, even minor ones, need to come directly from the sponsor. The first step is realizing when you have a leader with an ego that could harm their own project. Don't be afraid to ask your sponsor or line manager for support, as they may have helpful insights.

Step up. If a project leader has a huge ego, and you're in a position to do so, you will need to step up and meet the challenge. While *"servant leadership"* can be a wonderful approach, when egos are in charge, stepping up with confidence will drive the respect required to navigate this tough terrain and lead the team to win. It helps to discuss the people-side dynamics with your team, to protect them and yourself. Otherwise, the team may find they are approached to do things differently and against the best interests of the project, and not know how to respond. Establish and reinforce communication pathways to avoid undermining anyone. And if you're the project manager, be sure you have a leader who can help when you need to escalate.

Beware of Trojan Horses (or Rabbits). In these situations, be cautious of people who are like friendly rabbits. They may have been sent by the egotistical leader to case the joint. Everyone loves fluffy bunnies, but be careful particularly when you're desperate to make the project work. Bunnies could be brats who are destructive and misdirect you.

 PRESENTED BY...

ROSALIND GUY

Rosalind Guy is the founder of *Unboxed Insights*, through which she provides Fractional and Interim leadership.

She partners with leaders, executives, business owners, and transformational teams to uncover what's really happening beneath the surface of their business, people, and leadership – and turn those insights into clarity, traction, and tangible results.

A seasoned speaker and advisor, Rosalind is often found on podcasts, panels, and stages, weaving in stories of resilience and transformation, including the time she signed up for the 2015-2016 Clipper Round the World Yacht Race with no sailing experience and returned a circumnavigator.

With over two decades of senior leadership experience across SaaS, fintech, payroll, and global service delivery, Rosalind built and led high performing Project Management Office *(PMO)*, Service Delivery, and transformation teams on three continents, scaled operating models, and steered organizations through growth, restructuring, and reinvention. She brings that same focus and calm to her advisory roles, fractional leadership portfolio, and to her speaking engagements, where she shares her insights.

Passionate about emerging technology and AI, she never turns down a *"nerdy"* conversation, especially when it unlocks new ways of thinking or practical application.

Beyond business, she serves her community as a trustee at her local community center and delivers AI sessions for the M3 Job Club, helping professionals navigate career transitions.

Now firmly on dry land in Hampshire, UK, Rosalind shares her home with two mischief-makers—TC the tabby cat and Mitzy the Miniature Schnauzer—who remain unimpressed by her love of innovation *(and her calendar)*.

Learn more about Rosalind and her work at www.unboxedinsights.com

This final section focuses on the art of engaging stakeholders, managing sponsors, and communicating with impact.

You'll find valuable strategies for navigating change, building productive relationships, and delivering results through authentic collaboration.

Herding Cats
A Projectland Production

ACT III

CHAPTER 17

CHECK YOUR EGO AT THE DOOR

Change Enablement in High-Powered Teams *(The Greatest Night in Pop)*

The Greatest Night in Pop
Logline: "On January 28th, 1985, dozens of the era's most popular musicians gathered in Los Angeles to record a charity single for African famine relief. Setting egos aside, they collaborated on a song that would make history."[20]

SETTING THE SCENE

THE GREATEST NIGHT IN POP IS A DOCUMENTARY ON THE production of the song, *"We Are the World"*—chronicling the process and production of recording a song with 47 of the most popular voices of the time, together in one night, all in the name of change. The team leaders consisted of some of the biggest names in music: Quincy Jones *(producer, big picture thinker)*, Lionel Ritche *(co-writer and project manager)*, and Michael Jackson *(co-writer and subject matter expert)*.

The vision for the project began with Harry Belafonte. Belafonte was not just a singer and actor. He was an activist. He was a major voice of the Civil Rights Movement in the US and championed rights in Africa since his first visit in 1963. A large part of Mr. Bellefonte's mission was to use music and his artistry to create a movement. He brought calypso music to an international audience and spent years working on various social and political issues on the African continent. The idea to release a song to raise money for famine relief in Africa, came from a fellow antipoverty activist from the United Kingdom *(UK)*, Bob Geldof.

The leadership team's view of change led them to organically model change enablement before the term existed. Their approach of change enablement and its role is how *The Greatest Night in Pop* achieved transformational success, creating world change. They knew that people matter in all phases of the project, from kickoff to closing. They recognized the importance of knowing the players and understanding the team. They inherently knew that change enablement means not only operating without fear of change, but embracing it by providing the team with information, resources, and support.

At the end of the movie, a caption sums up the impact:

"Since the release, 'We Are the World' has raised over $80 million (equivalent to approx. $160 million in 2024) for humanitarian causes in Africa and continues to raise money to this day."

According to *United Support of Artists for Africa*, more than 500 African organizations in 21 African countries have received funding from the *"We Are the World"* project[21]. Marcia Thomas, Executive Director of USA for Africa, says, ***"They could not have known that, 35 years later, their actions would have helped inspire change in the world, one caring person at a time."***[22]

> "It's still the anthem that brings hope to a lot of people. That song is the anthem we were looking for."
>
> — Lionel Richie[23]

HOT TAKE: Transformational leaders who employ people-first, change enablement strategies can even keep divas focused on achieving desired outcomes under tight timelines.

 THE MOVIE MOMENT[S]

While I was fascinated by the whole movie, the following scenes stood out to me as wonderful examples of situations we often face on projects, and lessons for how we might handle them.

CHECK YOUR EGO AT THE DOOR

After months of recruiting the biggest names in the business, the night arrived, January 28, 1985. Lionel Ritchie has just hosted the American Music Awards and celebrities are making their way to the famous A&M Studios. Michael Jackson skipped the awards show to be first at the studio laying down vocals, handling logistics, and putting final touches on the song. Before the singers arrive, Quincy Jones grabs a black magic marker and hastily scribbles on a simple sheet of paper. He tapes it above the only entrance to A&M Studios. An impromptu sign posted for each celebrity to see: *"Check Your Ego at the Door."* They had been told the project was artist only. Each celebrity arrived alone—no glam squad, no entourage.

THE POWERFUL KICKOFF

Bob Geldof's opening remarks cut through the hubbub of excited celebrities mingling, happy to see old and new friends and to meet their icons. He addresses the group fresh off his trip, where he had raised money for anti-famine relief in Ethiopia.

"To put you in the mood of the song you are about to sing," he says, *"which hopefully will save millions of lives . . ."* He goes on to explain what he has witnessed on the continent and relates it to the mission and purpose of the project. The room falls silent, the buzz from meeting and greeting fellow icons fades to a sacred place—unified and focused under one common goal. He asks them to put what they're feeling into the song. He concludes with *"Thanks everybody. Let's hope it works."* No one knew if their idea would work or not.

THE THING ABOUT TROUBLEMAKERS

In one scene, the leadership team has been working diligently to record and produce the song AND music video in real time while keeping the team engaged. The song needed something else—a new lyric. Just when they're making progress, the inevitable happens—change!

Out of nowhere comes a voice singing, *"U-lim-wangu."* Lionel Ritchie looks stunned. The same voice sings, *"La-to-to."* Here comes trouble. The artists stir, as confusion hangs in the air. It is none other than Stevie Wonder. *"I think we should have some Swahili somewhere in the song,"* he offers. Then begins the chatter, the thoughts, the chaos. Ultimately one of the artists walks out, uncomfortable with speaking Swahili.

Wonder had some rationale behind his troublemaking. He was originally asked to co-write during the initiation phase but never answered the phone. Fast forward to the execution phase, and he wants his opinion to be heard. He saw his moment to provide input, and he took it. Ritchie works to stop the scope creep. It ends when someone mentions aloud to Ritchie and the group, *"They don't speak Swahili in Ethiopia."*

Geldof reappears to gently realign the group. *"There's no point in talking to the people who are starving,"* he says. *"We're talking to the people who have the money to give."* His view was that an unknown language would not speak to their audience. Worse, it could confuse them and turn them away. Wonder's potential scope creep of adding an additional language gives the group a moment to pause and think. It is 3am and they are running out of time to complete the song. The problem remains; a refrain is needed for the section in question.

The leadership team of Jackson, Jones, and Ritchie hold a brief side discussion. How can they enable the lyric change needed with minimum chaos, understanding their team?

Jones turns to the entire group and asks the one and only question posed to the group that night, *"Does everybody like the lyric, one world?"* There's resounding agreement from the artists.

Lionel Ritchie follows up, *"One world, Our children. One world, so let's start giving."*

And just like that, the adaptive, empowering, collaborative power of change enablement resolves the issue amicably.

 "ACTION!!!" PROJECTLAND SUCCESS TIPS

So many projects introduce change—a new way of working, a new product to support, or a new service to deliver. Some are even aimed at true transformation, like eliminating starvation. The problem is that most projects fail, and leading change is especially tricky.

Traditional change management on projects is strict, controlling, and moves from top down. It is hierarchical with a usually set, small group in charge of implementation, while everyone else is expected to follow. The intent is to minimize or avoid change. However, change is unavoidable. Can you imagine this style of change management implemented during a project involving some of the biggest celebrities, all volunteering their time and talent? What project leader wants to tell *"The Boss" (Bruce Springsteen)* he cannot make any changes without permission? Ha!

In contrast, *change enablement* provides people with the necessary information and support—alongside tools, processes, and strategies—to help them adapt and transition to change[24]. For example, though the group debated Stevie Wonder's proposed lyric change, Bob Geldof reminded everyone of the goals and target audience, giving them a strategy around which to create the missing lyric. From there, they could collaborate and produce material everyone could embrace. It is an enabling approach that focuses on giving people the means to change, understanding that change WILL happen. In comparison to traditional change management, the focus is adaptive and empowering with flexible responses. It is team-oriented and collaborative, and the intent is expective, empowered, and risk-ready.

Change enablement plays a role in how a project team views change, how *"issues"* like scope creep are handled, and how risks are addressed. Each of these roles was pivotal in the successful, transformative results of the *"We Are the World"* project.

Here are change enablement strategies that were evident in the movie moments above and can help you set your project up for transformational success, too.

Remember that people and processes go hand in hand. Understand your team as individuals and a group and tailor your process accordingly.

Quincy Jones set the tone with his handwritten *"Check your ego at the door"* sign, and it was a brilliant change enablement strategy. The idea was for the atmosphere to be collaborative. A place where egos are literally left at the door and the individual celebrities are open and ready to adapt *(the definition of change enablement)*—becoming a team in the name of the project. Only allowing artists in the room left the celebrities to interact with one another without outside influence—they were less likely to be difficult and hide amongst the familiarity of their own personal staff. This disarmed the biggest stars in music, putting them in the best position to come together. Plus, it humanized them, setting the stage for the kickoff and tying their own humanity to the humanity of the project.

Focus on value delivery. Good project leaders provide direction, purpose, and a culture for the project and its people that is focused on the ultimate goal *(in this case, raising money)*. This helps to navigate and embrace change requests and transitions without getting thrown off course.

The kickoff masterfully set the tone of direction, purpose, and culture in a collaborative fashion, tying the humanity of the top artists of 1985 with everyday Ethiopians suffering from famine. Inviting Geldof to lead the kickoff was another brilliant change enablement strategy. Since Geldof was tied to a slightly similar and successful project in the UK with the same goal, he enabled the team with the information and support needed to help them adapt and transition into the project. As a result, he was able to redirect the team's attention toward the goal and the target audience when debates occurred. This was another powerful technique for creating the positive project culture needed to work through pitfalls that are inevitable in Projectland.

Create an adaptive and collaborative view of change. Rather than taking a top-down approach, be team oriented and collaborative. This mindset shift can make the difference between a chaotic and transformative culture.

Change enablement methods incorporate two key steps: prepare for the inevitable changes and understand your team. With *"We Are the World,"* the project team leaders were well aware of the type of dynamic change inherent to projects of this nature—as well as what it would be like to manage and work with this particular group of star players, being artists and managers themselves. Choosing enablement means embracing change and understanding the behaviors, norms, and motivations of those invited—individually and as a group. This choice is significant.

Implement change enablement. Focus on developing an adaptive, empowering, and flexible response to disruptors or outliers that will rear their heads on occasion. The intent is to be proactive, empowered, and risk ready.

Sometimes troublemakers are also known as change makers, but not always. When Stevie *"Troublemaker"* Wonder introduces the idea of adding Swahili lyrics, the leadership team quickly adapts, offers gentle guidance, and engages the team in determining the best way forward. Sometimes suggestions that at first seem disruptive can make a positive difference in the end result when handled appropriately. On the surface, adding Swahili lyrics sounded quite appropriate, but in the context of the target audience, and combined with the fact that Ethiopians don't speak Swahili, it was rightfully dismissed in favor of something the team could align around—the *"one world, our children, let's start giving"* concept.

📣 DIRECTOR'S COMMENTS

The Greatest Night in Pop turns a real project journey into a thrilling adventure and one that I've known all my life. I am the youngest of five siblings. Each were born two years apart until I arrived five years after the fourth child. Surprise! Life was not easy for our family, living in a housing project in the South Bronx, New York.

To navigate this environment, we had to think on our feet and find the best-case scenario, where we existed safely with as little monetary loss, physical harm, and mental anguish as possible. I learned to read people and situations early and quickly for my own survival—within the household and outside of it—whether defending myself, my family, or an individual member of it. I was curious, turning the act of survival into a continuous learning and growth experience.

Finding solutions, the best route to take without further loss *(and with possible elevation)* gave me a sense of pride and accomplishment. In project management terms, my risk management skills, ability to process, plan, execute, and adapt, based on the stakeholders and power players *(e.g., landlord, various authorities and institutions)* is what got me recognized in my family and promoted to **"family project manager."**

Fast forward some years… I had just completed the Google PM course and started studying for the Project Management Professional *(PMP)* certification. I was drowning in concepts and terms. Fortunately, my strengths include curiosity, being a philomath *(a lover of learning)*, and developing people. I love applying newly learned concepts to various areas of life, culture, and industries. Application is the sum of retention and impact, which is how I know when I've truly mastered the concept.

Watching this documentary helped me to apply, organize, and make connections to what I was learning. It reminded me that learning can be entertaining and culturally relevant.

I saw myself and my life in what was depicted. My worlds collided. I was a child when this song was released. I remember the video, Michael Jackson, the blue and red font of the logo, and the excitement around it all. Now, I was able to travel back in time and relive it with fresh eyes, through a refined adult lens and a project management brain.

I saw each movie moment illustrating change enablement, and I realized that I learned firsthand growing up how change enablement can shift lives. While I was too young to be too stressed, but aware enough to be concerned, I worked to unify my family, keep them calm, informed, and empowered. Curiosity drove me to be adaptive, predictive, and collaborative, not risk avoidant in the face of strict, controlled processes and a hierarchical system. That gave us—as a unit and individuals—just enough energy to make transformational changes.

I felt like I was watching one of the greatest project managers in action. Lionel Ritchie said his job was to solve any problems on the floor. *"I'm walking around to each little camp, putting out fires."* He centered the people, including the troublemakers, well before change enablement existed as a concept. This touched me on several levels. People are the key. Their view of change is key. And that is how you not only run a project, but also how you impact and create high-level change in the world—transformational success.

REALITY SHOW: WHEN LIFE IMITATES ART

I worked as a third-party consultant with the U.S. Environmental Protection Agency *(EPA)*, which, among other things, identifies and assesses Superfund sites. These are locations across the United States that are contaminated with hazardous waste that are to be cleaned up under the Comprehensive Environmental Response, Compensation, and Liability Act *(CERCLA)*. The goal is to significantly reduce waste and health risks and hopefully return the site to productive use. The work included multiple stakeholders on several levels, all with their own goals and stakeholders.

TRYOUTS

My work was centered around *"Tryouts,"* where residents could try out as candidates to be considered for opportunities to learn, train, and hopefully work on the contaminated sites within their community. I was responsible for various parts of the project management, operations and facilitation, including managing the tryout process and the candidate selection. We relied on evaluators for activity and candidate feedback during the selection process. Evaluators were stakeholders who often held a percentage of jobs for the candidates.

The bigger picture is change. Our job was changing a contaminated location back to productive use in the community and economy, while changing the lives of residents by gainfully employing them. We needed to ensure the cleanup efforts would be done well and taken seriously, and who better to do so than the residents? As a facilitator, I helped all parties *(e.g., my colleagues at the EPA, the residents, and the evaluators)* to be empowered and understand the truth of the situation and what was at stake.

When I first joined Tryouts, the boundaries between what was shared with candidates and evaluators weren't clear. To better understand the process, I attended every stage, introduced myself to stakeholders, and observed both candidates and community organizations. From these conversations, I recognized the need to unify expectations.

On the day of Tryouts, I convened a mini-kickoff with evaluators, emphasizing that residents should be seen as true candidates, not just numbers. We then held a joint session with candidates and evaluators. Many participants assumed the program was only about certifications or temporary jobs, so I invited the EPA representative to explain the Superfund site's history and highlighted why local involvement in cleanup mattered. I also shared how training could lead to lasting opportunities.

By centering transparency, purpose, and empowerment, participants left not only with readiness and skills, but also with renewed energy and a shared vision. The experience became more than a project milestone—it was a catalyst for real change. Witnessing the true domino effect of change enablement and transformational success was as magical as 47 superstars coming together on the greatest night in pop.

🎬 "IT'S A WRAP!"

Here are three quick summary lessons that I hope will help you tackle your version of Projectland.

- **Traditional change management is not enough.** The strict, controlled, and hierarchical process of change management is usually risk avoidant. Find places where it makes sense to center, unify, and empower your team. This makes the transitions of change less detrimental to your project. Change enablement's form of risk-readiness makes the difficulty of transitions a team effort. You're not alone, rigidly hoping changes don't happen. You expect them, and your team is right behind you.
- **Change is inevitable.** Mindset is the key. Don't fear change. You are exerting enough energy on your projects; you don't need to hold your breath too. Lean on your risk management plan. When you've prepared your team with the tools and information to handle change with you, everyone can feel more confident and breathe a little easier.
- **Know your team. Prepare to win.** Do you know who you're working with? Meet with them as a team. Have one-on-one conversations. Ask them what they really love to do or love about the project and prepare to leverage it to build rapport, build the team, and enhance the project. Do you know who

the *"troublemakers"* are? What can you do to be proactive and address their concerns or have a plan for keeping the team focused? The better you know your team, the better prepared you are to beat the odds and win.

🎬 PRESENTED BY…

ROSALIN ALEXIS WALCOTT

Rosalin Alexis Walcott is the founder and principal project manager of Olivienne Spencer Consulting and Tethered Hearts Collective.

A solution-driven project manager specializing in legal and environmental services, Rosalin coordinates multi-million-dollar transactions across the U.S. as a Commercial Real Estate Paralegal, while simultaneously advocating for youth through her transformative work. As a dynamic speaker and 2023 Awardee of the Women of Project Management Community Impact Award, she stands at the forefront of industry leadership.

Rosalin serves as a Community Builder and Development Strategist, guiding youth through their journey to adulthood via Tethered Hearts Collective – an online resource community for those thrust into adulting without support.

Her project management expertise spans 10 years as a consultant, including pivotal work alongside the Environmental Protection Agency *(EPA Superfund Site Job Training Initiative)* as selection process developer and facilitator. She has traveled to Superfund Sites around the U.S., preparing local residential candidates for environmental remediation and cleanup-related careers.

This work ignites her passion for history, people management and development, program building, and facilitation. Beyond her professional pursuits, she channels creativity through writing, photography, traveling and music, while spending time hiking, biking and trying to visit every national park she can.

Empathy is her engine. Empowerment is her brand.

Driven by purpose, grounded by impact, and always building with love.

CHAPTER 18

"I'M MAKING THIS UP AS I GO"

Leading on Purpose *(Raiders of the Lost Ark)*

RAIDERS OF THE LOST ARK
Logline: "In 1936, archaeologist Indiana Jones is tasked by Army Intelligence to help locate a legendary ancient power, the Ark of Covenant, before the Nazis get it first."[25]

SETTING THE SCENE

THE MOVIE TAKES PLACE DURING WORLD WAR II. INDIANA Jones is a famous archaeologist recruited by the US government to locate the Ark of the Covenant—a legendary chest said to contain the stone tablets of the Ten Commandments, brought down from Mount Sinai by Moses as described in the Old Testament. The Ark is said to wield great power, and the United States military wants to get to it before the Nazis do.

During the movie, Jones follows a highly successful plan and successfully navigates the risks that appear along the way.

He recovers an ancient artifact needed to locate the Ark from a former colleague's daughter.

He uses the artifact to determine the precise location of the Ark.

He hires a team to exhume the Ark and successfully retrieve it from its ancient underground resting place.

This is where the plan falls apart. As soon as he retrieves the Ark, the Nazis find him and steal it. Through a series of daring escapades, Jones evades capture, but not before the Nazis crate the Ark and send it off in a truck guarded by a convoy of soldiers.

His plans have completely gone off the rails. His resources are almost non-existent. And, he's literally up against an army. Normal people give up at this point. What keeps him going?

In movie terms, it's called a *MacGuffin*. It's the object, event, or character that motivates the characters and drives the story forward. You can always tell what the MacGuffin is in an Indiana Jones movie because it's built right into the title—e.g., *Lost Ark, Temple of Doom, Last Crusade, Crystal Skull, Dial of Destiny*.

Ever since he was a child, Indiana Jones has had a passion for the history contained in archaeological artifacts. It's what drives him toward his goal even when his carefully laid plans have completely fallen apart.

It is his purpose!

> **HOT TAKE:** When things don't go according to plan (and they rarely do), keep your project on track by having a powerful purpose.

THE MOVIE MOMENT

As the scene begins, we find Indiana Jones hiding on an embankment in the desert with his long-time friend, Salah, and his love interest, Marion. They are overlooking the chaos at the site of the archeological dig where the Ark was discovered, and the Nazi convoy is leaving the site with the coveted artifact. Jones, also known as Indy, is clearly agitated, and his companions are looking to him for direction on what to do next.

"Get back to Cairo" he says. *"Get me some kind of transport to England. Boat… plane… anything. Meet me at Omar's. Be ready for me."* He turns away. *"I'm going after that truck!"*

Salah asks, *"How?"*

Indy turns back and replies *"I don't know, I'm making this up as I go."*

He sets off in pursuit of the Nazi truck carrying the Ark. After another series of unplanned, courageous, life-threatening escapades, he recovers the Ark. The Nazis, however, steal it back again and put it on a submarine. Undeterred, Indy relentlessly pursues the Ark, refusing to give up even as his plan unravels, until he finally achieves his goal and delivers the Ark to the United States.

🎬 "ACTION!!!" PROJECTLAND SUCCESS TIPS

Here are a couple of realities you'll have to face in Projectland:

Things won't always go according to plan. If they did, we wouldn't call it a project, we'd call it a miracle.

When things don't go according to plan, you need to have a way to keep yourself and your team focused. This is what having a clearly defined, meaningful, and powerful purpose—a MacGuffin—can do.

As detailed in their report, *Maximizing Project Success: Elevating the impact of the Project Profession. Elevating the impact on our world*, the Project Management Institute *(PMI)* recently completed a study that resulted in a new, practical definition of project success:

Delivered value that was worth the effort and expense.

Previous definitions have focused more on achieving schedule and budget targets as the most important measures of project success. Fortunately, there is now emphasis on the desired project outcome—or MacGuffin—as the most important measure of success. On-schedule and on-budget don't matter if you don't deliver value, but if you DO deliver the value—schedule and budget can become less important.

📣 DIRECTOR'S COMMENTS

The appeal of the Indiana Jones character is that he represents the exact opposite of everything that's natural to me. I am organized. I like structure. I like plans. I like checklists. I have checklists for everything. One of my checklists is a list of all my other checklists. But deep inside, I crave the mystery and excitement that shows up in the movie, and I long for that kind of adventure in both my professional and personal life.

Structure and organization are a good starting point for a career in project management, but as I found out, not nearly enough to be truly successful.

Early in my career I progressed nicely along the project management track. My organizational skills worked well in the Information Technology *(IT)* support operations area I managed, so I was given an opportunity to take on project work.

Organizational skills continued to help me get ahead, and I pursued, and successfully attained, the Project Management Professional *(PMP)* certification. After that, I set my sights on a promotion. To my chagrin, my manager had a frank conversation with me. She said ***"You're really organized, and you get things done, but you have a reputation for being*** book smart on project management. Your forms, templates, and checklists are useful for the other project leaders, but we don't necessarily know if you could handle the unpredictability of the large, complex projects we'd normally assign to a senior project leader."

Ouch.

To really get ahead, I felt like I had to become the *"Indiana Jones"* of project management—able to adapt to barrels rolling toward me. So, at the next opportunity, I decided to change my approach.

REALITY SHOW: WHEN LIFE IMITATES ART

With my desire for promotion in mind, I was assigned to a project to implement a manufacturing system for a new product line that would be made in our flagship plant in Minnesota's St. Croix Valley. This was important not just to the company, but to the community. The great recession of 2008 had resulted in massive layoffs, and our company's reputation for being an employer of choice was at risk. This new product would help drive increased sales in a new market, and as a result, *bring jobs back to the valley.*

I poured all my project management *"book smarts"* into it. I set up team meetings, built out the detailed work plan, scheduled stakeholder updates, and got the project rolling.

Did things go according to plan? Absolutely not. It went off the rails—early and often. Vendor delays resulted in equipment arriving later than planned, which meant we had to rearrange our software component priorities. Also, the new product line didn't fit neatly into our product configuration models and required significant customization. On top of all that, we hired a lot of new people to get the project off the ground, so we were trying to do the impossible with an inexperienced team.

Meanwhile, the manufacturing engineering team had just implemented new manufacturing technology that our project's systems had to integrate with—we're talking robots and lasers.

So, what is a project manager to do? I met with everyone again. We replanned. And negotiated tradeoffs. And rearranged priorities. And broke a lot of my own rules about maintaining plans and resisting scope change. It was by far the most challenging chapter in my career to date.

What kept me going, and what I kept using to motivate the team, was the concept of bringing jobs back to the valley—that was our MacGuffin. Growing up in the St. Croix Valley and working at the same company my dad worked at for nearly 40 years made this particularly meaningful to me.

In the end, after all the adaptation and re-planning, we installed the assembly lines, implemented the systems, and went live. Overall, the project was a year late and the system costs were almost double what was budgeted. This isn't something I'd normally brag about, but ultimately, we delivered the value that our business wanted—and at the end-of-year employee town hall meeting, our executive vice-president used the words *"flawless execution"* to describe the project.

I muzzled my inner perfectionist and stayed silent rather than arguing with him. Instead, I quoted him in my performance appraisal that year, and got the elusive promotion I had been looking for. Most importantly, we brought jobs back to the valley.

I continued to work on the new product line program for the next several years. It wasn't clear to me how much I had changed my work approach to be more purpose-driven and adaptive until I had another project go off the rails.

We had to develop an extremely complex enhancement that impacted two manufacturing plants. This was just the latest in a seemingly endless series of product line improvements, driven by a business unit leader with an insatiable appetite for new ways to market the product.

We were trying to deliver multiple in-scope features, our engineers kept changing product designs, and our development teams were exhausted from overwork. The environment had become toxic. In fact, one of my team members had a heart attack and was out of work for six weeks during this time.

I presented this situation—along with options and tradeoffs—as part of my proposal for corrective action to that same demanding business sponsor. My recommendation was to delay the go live date by 3 months.

The product line director was silent for a while, then sighed deeply, and pointed at my timeline chart and said, **"Well that's untenable."**

To this date I don't know what the word *"untenable"* means, and I REFUSE to look it up. I do know what it *doesn't* mean—it doesn't mean, **"Please proceed with your recommendation."** He finished up the conversation by saying **"You know, Mike, you keep coming in here every week talking about these risks, but then, you keep doing it. Your team keeps delivering."**

Dead silence.

He was right. This team was awesome—I couldn't argue with him on that point.

The thing is, I had a feeling that he would react that way. Before I even went into the meeting, my team had already been working on how they were going to meet the deadline, what they were going to trade off, and how they were going to modify our approach. We found an additional developer who had some free time, identified a temporary workaround in the code that we could implement, and worked a little more overtime. Given the team's exhaustion, it wasn't the relief I asked for, but by constantly readjusting to the situation, we made it through.

I started to think, *"Maybe I am like Indiana Jones. Maybe I don't need a fully blown detailed plan that we follow to a T for every project. I don't have a whip and a gun, but maybe I just need the project manager's version—an adventurer's mindset and a powerful MacGuffin."* I decided that I just have to own this new purpose-driven and adaptive approach.

So that's what I do now. I love to plan, and I love to have a half dozen back up plans, and I usually do. But where I experience the most success is outside the plan, outside the box—where the magical power of purpose drives the impossible forward.

"IT'S A WRAP!"

It's great to have a plan. And a backup plan. And another backup plan. But it's also important to remember that nothing ever goes quite the way you planned, and when you take on the role of project manager, that's what you sign up for.

More than a plan, what drives you and your team forward no matter what happens is a powerful purpose—a MacGuffin. My experience has shown me that when you have a clear purpose, the plans practically create themselves.

PRESENTED BY...

MICHAEL SCHAFER, PMP

After nearly four decades of leading projects, processes, and people in the realms of manufacturing, software development, and IT infrastructure, Mike recently left the corporate world to embark on a new venture. He co-founded *Back in the Box Consulting*, with a mission to empower clients through straightforward, principle-centered, step-by-step solutions to common project, communication, and leadership challenges. By doing so, he liberates their creative energy, allowing them to focus on groundbreaking, *"out of the box"* work.

Mike makes his home in the beautiful St. Croix River Valley in Minnesota, where he enjoys life to the fullest. He's a proud father of four adult children, a master martial artist, an enthusiastic sailor, a decent skier, an occasional cyclist, and, naturally, a passionate movie-goer.

CHAPTER 19

SPARED NO EXPENSE

Managing Your Sponsor Without Getting Eaten *(Jurassic Park)*

JURASSIC PARK
Logline: "An industrialist invites some experts to visit his theme park of cloned dinosaurs. After a power failure, the creatures run loose, putting everyone's lives, including his grandchildren's, in danger."[26]

SETTING THE SCENE

JOHN HAMMOND, CEO OF INGEN, *(PLAYED BY RICHARD ATtenborough)* walks into an archaeology trailer at a dig site and pops a bottle of champagne that he finds in the fridge. Hammond has come to recruit Dr. Allen Grant *(Sam Neill),* a leading paleontologist, and Dr. Ellie Sattler *(Laura Dern),* a leading paleobotanist, to join his review team of experts. Grant and Sattler are none too pleased that this strange visitor has opened the bottle of champagne they'd been saving, but Hammond has a good reason to celebrate. Hammond excitedly goes on to introduce himself *(he's one of their top financial backers)* and describes his idea.

"I've got an island off the coast of Costa Rica," he says. "I've leased it from the government, and I've spent the last five years setting up a kind of... biological preserve. Really spectacular... Spared no expense." He goes on to explain that he's gathered some of the most influential experts in their fields to build his dream of a dinosaur adventure park. When they politely decline, he promises to fund their dig for another three years. That changes everything.

Hammond brings Grant and Sattler, along with skeptical chaos theorist Ian Malcom *(Jeff Goldblum)* and **"bloodsucking"** lawyer Donald Gennaro to his remote island. And from the moment he utters those famous words, **"Welcome to Jurassic Park,"** the team is off on an exciting thrill ride. That is, until things go very wrong. To make matters worse, Hammond's grandkids are along for the journey.

> **HOT TAKE:** A rich and powerful sponsor supporting your project with excitement and resources is a blessing – and can also be a curse.

THE MOVIE MOMENT

Dr. Alan Grant and Dr. Ellie Sattler are overlooking herds of dinosaurs roaming the valley below when Dr. Grant asks, **"How did you do this?"** Hammond smiles and says, **"Let me show you."**

He gives them a behind-the-scenes tour and sends them off on an automated vehicle ride through the park. What he doesn't realize is that his IT guy, Dennis Nedry *(Wayne Knight)*, has made a deal with an opposing company, and when Nedry arranges to shut down the park's security for a moment while he steals the dino embryos, everything turns to chaos. A storm comes. Nedry gets eaten by a dinosaur. The electric gates have been deactivated. And now a T-Rex is loose near the tour vehicles.

With his grandkids and guests in danger, Hammond is sitting at a table with Ellie Sattler, who has somehow made it back to headquarters. As a storm rages outside, electricity and security systems fail all over the park and dinosaurs run amok. Hammond realizes that he has lost control. Hammond and Sattler stress-eat the exquisite ice cream that's melting, to which Hammond mutters sadly, but ironically, that he **"spared no expense."**

"ACTION!!!" PROJECTLAND SUCCESS TIPS

John Hammond is clearly the project sponsor for Jurassic Park. He never fails to provide resources, and he always lets everyone around him know that the park was his idea. He's excited about it and willing to share that excitement with everyone.

In essence, he's the project's cheerleader, he has money, and he is not afraid to spend it. In Projectland, Hammond is the King of his Jurassic Park Jungle. But for a successful project, is passion and resources enough?

Consider this: How many times does Hammond utter the words *"spared no expense?"* Don't look on the Internet. The answer is below.

First, during the invitation to Drs. Grant and Sattler, in their archaeologists' trailer, he promises to fund their archeologist dig for another three years and boasts how he's spared no expense for this fantastic endeavor.

Second, during a lunch meeting with major stakeholders, Hammond is discussing the park's attractions, and he reminds them that he spared no expense.

Third, before the tour of Jurassic Park, Hammond gleefully describes the features of the new driverless electric Ford Explorer, sharing that he spared no expense. Note: Jurassic Park was released in 1993, this was years before electric or driverless cars would become prevalent.

Fourth, Hammond once again boasts that he spared no expense while giving a tour of the automated control room from which the entire park could be operated.

Fifth, when he shares his ice cream with Sattler while the rest of the group is in danger, he can't help but boast about the premium ice cream, once again uttering that he spared no expense.

But even he realizes at this point that all that spending was meaningless amidst everything that went wrong. They solemnly discuss the lack of control and Hammond muses on what would be different next time *(Sattler is likely wondering,* **"Next time!?"***)*. Note: Even though Hammond is not a project manager, he is using a project management technique for capturing *"lessons learned"* project data.

Unfortunately, despite all his riches and passion, Hammond's expertise or interest didn't appear to include Information Technology *(IT)*. And here comes a paradox in the movie: Hammond, who spared no expense, only hires one IT person. Not only is there only one IT person, but it appears to be the cheapest IT person to bid on the project. At one point, Nedry argues with Hammond about his lack of pay for his ability. How many times have we seen this in projects!? The contract is awarded to the lowest bidder, not necessarily the one with the best qualifications; then we are surprised when, lo and behold, problems ensue.

Aside from his blind spot around the IT requirements, Hammond exemplifies the power of the sponsor role with key characteristics, including:

- **Providing and securing resources** – Throughout the movie, Hammond reminds everyone of his generosity in funding the project.
- **Engaging as top project spokesperson and cheerleader** – He continuously and excitedly pitches his ideas and showcases the park's fantastic features.
- **Leading Actively** – He recruits experts personally and is involved in the entire project from beginning to end, including research, construction, entertainment, dinosaur life, and more.
- **Accepting Accountability** – At the end of the movie, Hammond realizes he did not have control over the whole situation when his grandchildren were lost in his park with dinosaurs.

This is a perfect example why even the best project sponsors can benefit from a trained project manager *(and perhaps a steering team)* to overcome their blind spots and broadly examine the goals from all stakeholder perspectives.

A project manager is never mentioned in the movie; perhaps one could have prevented this dino-sized disaster. If there had been a project manager, managing this powerful sponsor would have been a critical skill. The sponsor and project manager need to establish a positive working relationship to lead the project as a unified team, which can be accomplished by:

- **Establishing the Three Rs**
    - Relationship - Build a strong working relationship by understanding the sponsor's personality and what drives them, their strengths, weaknesses, and preferences.
    - Roles - Define role expectations and how you will drive the project to success together.
    - Responsibilities – Be clear on who is responsible for what tasks.
- **Manage Sponsor Expectations** – The sponsor may not be used to working in Projectland, where the world is different from operations. The project manager must understand what sponsors expect and manage the project toward its goals.
- **Manage Sponsor Engagement** – While the project manager cannot control senior leaders, he or she can discuss and influence the sponsor's level of commitment and involvement. The

project manager can also design opportunities for the sponsor to provide the input they desire, as well as ensure the sponsor gets the information they need, when and how they need it.

Together, the sponsor and project manager are the project's leadership team and need to establish clear communication with key stakeholders. There is an old saying in communication that, *"You cannot not communicate."* Unfortunately, there is often silence between project leadership and stakeholders. The project manager needs to engage with the sponsor and establish a definitive communication plan to discuss information, status, expectations, and other project requirements.

> **BONUS TIP:** If Jurassic Park was in Projectland, what phase of the project would it be in? As project leaders, this story begins where we like to see our projects. It is done—the park is built. The dinosaurs are grown. It is time for a celebration. Hammond is proudly showing off his world. Thus, we are in the closing phase of the project as the movie opens.

Unfortunately, as many project managers know all too well, there is still much work that needs to be accomplished to close a project and to tie up loose ends. And what appeared to be a successful project can unfortunately quickly become a failure as the remaining tasks fall out of control. But often the root of these problems is early in the project, as John Hammond learned; they only start becoming evident later. As they say, projects fail at the beginning, not at the end. This is why a project manager needs to be diligent throughout the entire life cycle of the project.

📣 DIRECTOR'S COMMENTS

When I first heard the words, *"Welcome to Jurassic Park,"* they brought a sense of wonder and excitement as I was welcomed into the fantastic, fantasy work filled with many characters and wild creatures. Watching the movie for the first time, I was on the edge of my seat wondering what was going to happen.

It is much the same feeling when I start a new project or begin a new semester at Penn State. The future is filled with a sense of awe in this new adventure. Everyone involved is anticipating the new opportunity and imagining what the future looks like.

Hammond had a vision for the first dinosaur adventure park, but that isn't enough. It takes a good leader to help us reach the end goal, resolve issues, and keep everyone from being eaten by the project.

🎬 REALITY SHOW: WHEN LIFE IMITATES ART

I was a member of a technology project management team for a new client. The client team decided to hold a multi-day Joint Application Development (*JAD*) session to gather requirements for a new system. The project team consisted of the project sponsor, client project manager, over 25 users of various functional roles, two documentation specialists, and two computer programmers.

On the first day, much like Jurassic Park, problems escalated quickly and there was little focus on the goal of the project. Everyone looked to the project sponsor to answer questions and to provide directions. When the sponsor left the room to take an *"important"* phone call and was unavailable, the other stakeholders focused their attention on their specific system needs, which were not necessarily aligned with the project's goals.

I learned three things from this bumpy JAD experience that have stuck with me.

First, the sponsor has the power to influence the project team. During the meeting, everyone looked to the project sponsor to provide vision and clarity. He knew the product and what needed to be accomplished. He answered questions confidently, shared knowledge, and commanded a sense of control. Much like John Hammond in Jurassic Park, he was a powerful resource.

Second, always make sure you have the correct decision-maker involved at the right times. The meeting was going well until the sponsor left the room for over an hour. When he returned and reviewed the requirements gathered over the last hour, he informed everyone that they did not fulfill the purpose of this application. The team was frustrated as their hard work was simply erased from the board.

Third, stay focused on the ultimate goal. After the morning session, the programmers thought they had heard what they needed to know. So, they started coding. But they failed to notice that the conversation had gone in another direction. The programmers kept focusing on their screens and not on the changing requirements discussions. Couple this with the absence of the sponsor, and the result was a disastrous morning session.

The morning situation was much like Hammond and Nedry, whose focus on their own agendas brought disaster to Jurassic Park.

Fortunately, we were able to get the JAD session back on track. During lunch, the project management team met with the sponsor to nail down the project's vision. On the board, we wrote the project's goal. After lunch, the group was broken into teams. Each team worked on a sub-goal activity and then reported back to the entire group. When anyone went astray, we pointed to the main goal written on the board. Engaging the team in this way made a huge difference in aligning everyone toward the goal and setting the project up for success.

In contrast, not all projects get back on track. When I was young in my career, I was pulled from my other projects and assigned to a project for a new client. The project was highly visible, and the company wanted the best experts working on the project. This sounds a lot like Jurassic Park! Like Hammond, our project sponsor was visionary and very engaged. Unfortunately, the technology was not yet at the level of his vision. At every meeting, people kept bringing new ideas and technical devices, which sent the project spiraling backward. There was no clear sense of direction, control, or focus on the goal. Looking back, I realize that my company had too many leaders on the team without anyone assigned as a clear decision-maker or facilitator. Thus, the project flipped and flopped back and forth, because no one managed the changing requirements driven by the client sponsor.

I wish I could say that the project had a happy movie-like ending where we were all heroes riding off into the sunset. Unfortunately, it ends with a cliffhanger. Most of the leaders in the project, including myself, left the company for other adventures. Basically, we all jumped on a helicopter and left the island before the dinosaurs could eat us.

"IT'S A WRAP!"

Dr. Ian Malcolm *(Jeff Goldblum)* commented on the chaos in Jurassic Park: *"Life will find a way."* Similarly, projects are alive. They change, adapt, and need constant monitoring or they will eat you up. Project leaders must be in control and keep the team focused on the project's main goal.

I'm currently living in the house that my wife designed and that my father-in-law and I built. He was a career carpenter who built homes.

Fortunately, we communicated and worked well together. From the blueprints of the house, we knew the final goal. When I would start asking too many questions about future tasks and materials, he would simply say: *"That's on the next page."* This would keep us focused on the necessary tasks of the day.

When you find yourself in Projectland and you have a powerful sponsor who is supplying input, resources, and excitement to the project, remember that you can't be simply an order taker. There must be a strong project manager who establishes a positive relationship with the sponsor and can manage up. Clearly communicating expectations and ensuring that everyone is focused on the ultimate goal is the key to delivering the exciting results that were envisioned at the start.

PRESENTED BY...

JESSE MIDDAUGH, PMP, MSIS

Jesse Middaugh, PMP, MSIS, enjoys education, people, and outdoor adventures. He has over 25 years of experience teaching classes in Information Science and Technology and Project Management as Assistant Teaching Professor at Penn State University *(Harrisburg campus)*. He is also the baseball team's Faculty Mentor and Ice Hockey Club's Advisor.

He has professional project management experience including governmental, military, and corporate clients. Jesse has a background in writing proposals, analyzing requirements, and managing projects. He has worked for Computer Sciences Corporation *(CSC)*, Price Waterhouse/Coopers, IBM, and other consulting companies. Also, Jesse has managed his own consulting company.

Jesse is an active member of PMI *(Project Management Institute)*. He was on the Board of Directors for the PMI-Keystone chapter for eight years; six of those years as the President. He also served as an international judge for the project management section of the F1 in Schools Competition (https://www.f1inschools.com/). Jesse volunteered with Lightshine Ministries (https://lightshineministries.org/) at Globe Creek, Alaska to build log cabins for a kid's camp (https://www.globecreekcamp.com/) and at Fairbanks Alaska, to assist with the World Eskimo Indian Olympics (https://www.weio.org/).

He and his wife, Joy, have been married for over 30 years and live near Harrisburg PA. They have two grown children and a Boston Terrier. Jesse is an avid baseball fan and roots for the Baltimore Orioles. He enjoys outdoor activities like fishing, archery and any sport. He traveled across the United State twice in an RV with his family, visiting over twenty different national parks and nearly every state in the country. Driving a camper across the country is a project and maybe a story for a later time.

CHAPTER 20

THE POWER OF AUTHENTIC RELATIONSHIPS

Rocking Stakeholder Engagement *(School of Rock)*

SCHOOL OF ROCK
Logline: "After being kicked out of his rock band, Dewey Finn becomes a substitute teacher of an uptight elementary private school, only to try and turn his class into a rock band."[27]

SETTING THE SCENE
THE FIRST THING YOU NEED TO KNOW ABOUT *SCHOOL OF ROCK* is that Dewey Finn *(Jack Black)* is an idiot. A loveable, hilarious idiot.

School of Rock is a hysterical, heart-warming film about a washed-up rock band artist, Dewey, making his comeback in the most unexpected way. After getting kicked out of his band shortly before an important competition, *Battle of the Bands*, Dewey sets off to start his own band. Dewey has been crashing on his friend Ned Schneebly's *(Mike White's)* couch for a long time to the great irritation of Ned's live-in girlfriend, Patty *(Sarah Silverman)*. Ned is also an ex-band member, but he has transitioned into an *"adult job"* as a substitute teacher. Patty is extremely uptight and critically domineering in the relationship with Ned.

After failed attempts to start a new band before the big *Battle of the Bands* competition, Dewey begins to wallow in his sorrows. While lounging at Ned's place, Dewey answers Ned's phone, and Principal Mullins *(Joan Cusack)* is on the other line. Principal Mullins works for Horace Green Preparatory School, and they are in desperate need of Ned, the substitute teacher with an excellent reputation. Assuming that Ned has answered the phone, she tells him the expected compensation which is very generous. Dewey seizes the opportunity to steal Ned's identity and become a substitute teacher at Horace Green.

Upon Dewey's arrival, after failing to correctly spell *"Mr. Schneebly,"* he tells the children to call him *"Mr. S."* Because he knows nothing about teaching and probably couldn't teach the provided subjects if he tried, he sends the kids on an endless recess. The kids meet him with all sorts of attitude. Some love endless recess, some would rather learn, but they all wind up with the same conclusion—*"Mr. S"* is a loser and they miss their full-time teacher. Until one day when everything changes...

All students at Horace Green are required to participate in music class. While in the restroom, Dewey hears the students' music class through the walls and, after washing his hands, runs down the hall to find the music room. Dewey's dancing eyebrows are awestruck at the students' musical talent, and he seizes the opportunity to start a new band with the students and return to his goal of entering the *Battle of the Bands*. The students were thrilled! Dewey assigns each student a role in the band perfectly suited to their skills and personality. Some played an instrument, some sang, others designed costumes, provided band security, or managed logistics.

The students' confidence skyrocketed as they worked hard to prepare for the *Battle of the Bands*. The young band encountered many obstacles: they faked illness so they could practice, lost trust in their leader, upset their parents and school staff, and at one point, faced the police! By the end of the movie, everyone learns valuable life lessons and becomes a better version of themselves.

> **HOT TAKE:** The most unlikely sources can teach you something powerful. Project leaders must foster an environment where everyone feels empowered to share their thoughts and ideas.

 THE MOVIE MOMENT

As the *Battle of the Bands* gets closer, it's time for Dewey to execute one of his most important tasks—gaining stakeholder buy-in. Dewey must win over Principal Mullins. Principal Mullins is a traditional, strict, rules-driven leader as demanded by the prominent preparatory school. She would not be easily convinced to support any activity that might disrupt the school day. Dewey's next move is nothing short of genius.

Dewey's passion for rock music helps him connect with others, and he leverages this passion in the scene I describe as, *"Would it be educational?"* The scene takes place in the most unlikely place to find Principal Mullins—a bar. She is utterly shocked when Dewey invites her to spend time with him after school hours; none of the teachers had ever included her in social events. She drinks her beer like a 17-year-old sneaking their first drink. With Stevie Nicks's hit, *"Edge of Seventeen"* playing in the background, Principal Mullins lets her guard down and reminisces about seeing Stevie in concert.

Once she's at ease, and half a pint in, Dewey successfully gets Principal Mullins to agree that Stevie *"is so much better live"*—the clever precursor to his next question: Can he take his students on a field trip to a concert? She responds by asking, *"Would it be educational?"* With great enthusiasm Dewey expertly tailors his pitch to share how the field trip aligns with her and the school's values and ensures it will be educational. He easily gains her buy-in. Success!

Dewey takes it a step further. After driving Principal Mullins back to the school, she has become so comfortable talking to him—thanks in part to the alcohol—that she opens up to him. Crying, she shares her anxiety caused by the stress of her job and that the pressure has turned her into someone she never wanted to be. As the tears flow, she claims she's not fun or funny anymore. Dewey assures her that she's wrong and comforts her with praise about how highly he thinks of her. Principal Mullins takes what he says to heart. It completely shifts her mood to one of positivity and gratitude. This is a huge step forward in their working relationship. Not only did Dewey secure buy-in for the field trip *(i.e., the Battle of the Bands)*, but he gained Principal Mullin's trust by simply being kind to her. Being kind and supportive goes a long way. And it shouldn't just come from leaders; it should come from everyone.

"ACTION!!!" PROJECTLAND SUCCESS TIPS

While I do not condone shmoozing a stakeholder with alcohol, committing identity theft, and lying, there are valuable lessons in how Dewey engages Principal Mullins.

ACTIVELY LISTEN TO STAKEHOLDER NEEDS, WANTS AND CONCERNS

Dewey listens to Principal Mullins's concerns and adapts his approach to make her comfortable and address her anxieties. He recognizes that, for her, the school's reputation and students' educational well-being are top priorities.

Project leaders are much more successful when they take the time to understand their stakeholders' perspectives, motivations, concerns, and goals.

BUILD RAPPORT THROUGH PERSONAL INTERESTS

When talking to a principal, you'd normally think of a school setting, but Dewey's invitation to take her out to a more relaxed, informal setting proved to be brilliant. The bar, the music, and his genuine friendly demeanor were the perfect combination for honest, open communication. He builds rapport by playing her favorite artist, Stevie Nicks, and expresses genuine interest in her personal life before diving into his ask.

Project leaders need to remember that stakeholders are human beings with passions and insecurities. It's important to get to know them on a human level to build strong relationships that will ultimately make the project more successful.

CUSTOMIZE COMMUNICATION TO FIT STAKEHOLDERS NEEDS

When Principal Mullins poses the question, *"Would it be educational?"*, Dewey's response, *"Would it be educational? It could be very educational,"* directly addresses her primary concern. His simple and completely honest answer makes Principal Mullins feel comfortable with allowing Dewey to take the kids to the concert.

It's also a great example of the mirroring technique, which is essentially active listening. It includes matching someone's physical actions and words, and even specifically repeating words or phrases to show you're paying attention. While Dewey may not have realized he was using the mirroring technique, his execution was flawless.

Adaptability is crucial. Effective stakeholder engagement means adjusting your message to meet your audience's priorities. By emphasizing benefits that align with stakeholder goals, project leaders can secure support more effectively. Stakeholders also appreciate when we get straight to the point in answering their questions. Of course, we should be honest too. And Dewey learns that lesson the hard way when Ned's girlfriend discovers that Dewey has stolen Ned's identity and calls the police, resulting in Dewey getting fired from Horace Green just before the *Battle of the Bands*. (Watch the movie to see how this situation unfolds!)

📣 DIRECTOR'S COMMENTS

This is one of my all-time favorite movies. It's the perfect blend of humor and an educational, feel-good story. While Dewey's actions aren't exactly a model of ethical behavior, his impact on others around him is undeniably positive. Dewey's *"stick it to the man"* mentality and passion for rock and roll reminds Ned how much he loves to play music and gives him confidence to end a toxic relationship. By recognizing the students' individual talents, inspiring confidence, and creating an environment where the students could express their concerns honestly, he helps them reach their full potential. In the end, the children's parents were proud and impressed. His ability to connect with Principal Mullins on a personal level highlights the power of genuine engagement.

In today's tech-driven world, building authentic relationships is becoming a lost art. Dewey's ability to connect over a shared love of music reminds us of the importance of *"the personal touch"* in professional interactions. Imagine starting your next meeting by asking everyone their favorite movie, concert, or song—or a tidbit about each other's backgrounds. You might be surprised how it fosters connection and collaboration. How might that foster connection and collaboration on your team?

🎥 REALITY SHOW: WHEN LIFE IMITATES ART

My friend Michael Schafer, a fellow contributing author, sees me as a master networker. I have worked hard to hone my ability to build strong relationships. As an *"introverted extrovert,"* I genuinely enjoy connecting with others but also treasure quiet time.

In my current remote role, I've prioritized building connections. Within my first five months, I've met over 100 colleagues across various departments, balancing work discussions with personal conversations. When talking to coworkers, I try to naturally bring up something not related to work. One of the easiest ways to do this in a remote environment is to comment on peoples' virtual backgrounds. By doing that, I've learned that one coworker is a mega Batman nerd, and another is passionate about indoor plants.

For those coworkers who don't use a virtual background, when it's appropriate, I'll make a comment about a pet in the background or the drink on their desk. People LOVE talking about their pets and I now have a fellow Pamplemousse-flavored-La-Croix-loving work buddy. *(If you've never had it and like bubbly water, do your taste buds a favor and drink one.)* Some of these connections have already become key stakeholders, others valuable resources, and a few have become new friends. By connecting with them on a personal level, it has made work easier and much more enjoyable.

🎬 "IT'S A WRAP!"

Dewey's unconventional approach to stakeholder engagement in *School of Rock* is an excellent example of what it may take to secure buy-in for a project. Obtaining stakeholder approval is one of the differentiating factors between project success or failure. By understanding Principal Mullins's priorities, building rapport, tailoring his message to her top concern, and fostering trust, Dewey wins her support for the field trip. These tactics are invaluable for project leaders facing their own stakeholder challenges.

Stakeholder engagement is about more than just presenting a compelling case—it's about listening, adapting, and creating an environment where stakeholders feel understood and respected. Like Dewey, project leaders can build relationships that inspire cooperation and commitment, ensuring project success.

Consider your network both inside and outside your workplace. To strengthen your network, you could make a list of ten people you'd like to meet and then reach out to them to schedule a friendly call. You never know how a relationship will affect your life—maybe they'll be a key stakeholder on one of your projects, maybe they'll become a trusted resource for brainstorming ideas, or maybe they'll become a close friend.

Most importantly, whenever you're in doubt, remember to…

Rock on, project rockstars!

🎬 PRESENTED BY...

RACHEL MUSSELL, PMP & DASM

Rachel Mussell brings expertise from managing dental equipment projects from procurement to installation, and managing a wide variety of marketing projects to her role at the Project Management Institute *(PMI)* where she is learning the ins-and-outs of professional educational product development. She is passionate about empowering individuals to reach their full potential by providing simple, actionable tools and techniques that drive success in both their professional and personal lives. For Rachel, every day is an opportunity to make a difference.

Whether managing projects or leading teams, Rachel thrives on empowering others. She is committed to creating safe, inclusive environments, facilitating networking, and hosting engaging learning sessions. Her ultimate goal is to inspire action, help others grow, and contribute to achieving organizational success—one small win at a time.

In addition to her work at PMI, Rachel is co-founder of *Back in the Box Consulting* with Michael Schafer, with a mission to empower clients through straightforward, principle-centered, step-by-step solutions to common project, communication, and leadership challenges. By doing so, Rachel and Mike release their clients' creative energy, allowing them to focus on groundbreaking, *"out of the box"* work.

Outside of *"Projectland,"* Rachel is an adventurer at heart. She loves spending time with her family, especially her pug Sami, whose charming grunts and snorts always light up a room.

CHAPTER 21

MASTERING THE ART OF NEGOTIATION

Lessons in Adapting, Listening, and Leverage *(Cash Out)*

Cash Out
Logline: "Professional thief Mason attempts his biggest heist with his brother, robbing a bank. When it goes wrong, they're trapped inside surrounded by law enforcement. Tension rises as Mason negotiates with his ex-lover, the lead negotiator."[28]

SETTING THE SCENE
THE MOVIE OPENS WITH A HIGH VALUE CAR THEFT GONE WRONG. After his partner in the heist and lover for two years, Amelia Decker *(played by Sex and the City's Kristin Davis)*, reveals herself to be an undercover FBI agent, heartbroken Mason *(John Travolta)*, the main character and lead negotiator,) retires to a peaceful life of fishing and beer—or so he thinks.

A mere three months later, his younger brother Shawn *(Lukas Haas)* asks him to lead a bank robbery. Mason declines, making it clear that he is finished with thievery.

But then, the phone wakes him from a nap. It's one of his former crew members, telling him the situation is bad and he needs to get on a plane; Shawn is currently attempting to lead the heist—a surefire failure.

Mason had always been the main planner and manager of the team, but this time he's coming in at the last minute with zero knowledge.

He flies out there and locates the bank, only to find his brother outside, already in the thick of things. Shawn is holding a gun toward a man's back. Mason starts coaching his brother and gathering intel. **"Stop looking around. Hide your gun. Who is this?"**

It's the bank manager.

Shawn says, *"Don't worry, it's an easy one. It's cut and dry."* To which Mason responds, *"If it looks cut and dry, it's not."*

He finds out that the crew is inside the bank, ready to go. Mason tells his brother to wait outside with the bank manager while he goes in to call off the heist. But then, the bank manager walks in with Shawn right behind him.

Things go sour very quickly thanks to Shawn's recklessness, and Mason takes over as lead. With customers still in the bank, the team ends up taking twenty-three hostages including staff and security.

The safety deposit box they're after turns out to be a trap set by the FBI. Local authorities, the FBI, SWAT teams, and Interpol surround the bank. None other than Amelia, Mason's ex, is sent as the FBI's negotiator.

> **HOT TAKE:** Negotiations are often the key to keeping a project on the rails and assuring stakeholder satisfaction—and the key to negotiation is leverage, i.e., what one party wants and what another party is willing to give.

🍿 THE MOVIE MOMENT

Mason, of course, needs to first understand the situation, as he has taken over planning on the spot.

With his nit-wit brother having employed his, *"You don't need a Plan B when Plan A is this good"* plan, which naturally led to a crisis, Mason enters negotiations with his back to the wall. Not only that, but he must negotiate with his ex-girlfriend, with whom he's still in love.

He begins by saying, *"I have a special request."* He asks Amelia to move everyone back fifty-feet from the bank. She does it, but she can't figure out why he asked for it. In reality, he is buying time.

She gets on the line again. He says he has another request, and since no harm has come to the hostages, she listens. This time he asks for pizza and drinks for everyone, and for her to deliver them personally, in under thirty minutes. She agrees.

She pulls the hand cart full of pizza and cases of water into the vestibule where the ATM is, and Mason stands inside the doorway to the bank, holding the door open halfway as they speak. He gathers more intel and says, *"I'm sorry for turning you into the pizza delivery girl, but it's the only way I could do a face-to-face, just you and me..."*

Her reply is that she is going to need two hostages and that's non-negotiable. And then, after that two every hour. He agrees quickly, which surprises Amelia. When she wheels the hand cart over to him, their hands overlap on the cart's handle and they seem to have a moment of connection.

He knows that the key to a good negotiation is leverage, which is what one party wants and what another party is willing to give. And in this case, he has the hostages and the FBI wants no harm to come to them. Fortunately, Mason doesn't want anything to happen to them or his crew either.

Meanwhile, when he discovers that the safe deposit box they were seeking was a decoy, he has to figure out what's really going on. He learns from the captive bank manager that the account numbers Shawn had tie to an adjacent building. This is where VIPs, particularly the owner of the box—powerful crime lord Abel Salazar—keep their secret files. The FBI wants what's in that box, and Amelia had no idea what her superiors had planned.

The mission has changed, and Mason must adjust while keeping the negotiations going.

"ACTION!!!" PROJECTLAND SUCCESS TIPS

Like Mason did in *Cash Out*, when you begin any type of negotiation, always learn as much as you can and start with the goal, even if the goal may evolve as more is known.

Let's break down seven key elements of negotiation, illustrate them with movie moments, and then see how this might play out in Projectland with an example project.

1. **Interests** – The underlying needs, desires, or concerns of each party.

Understanding interests leads to more creative and satisfying outcomes. In *Cash Out*, Mason was concerned about his only brother and his former crew going to jail or worse. Amelia was motivated to successfully negotiate a peaceful conclusion and prove herself to her superiors. And the invisible Abel Salazar, represented by his attorney, was interested in keeping his secrets private and away from the FBI.

2. **Positions** – The stated demands or stances that parties initially present.

While positions may seem to be rigid, they often mask the more flexible underlying interests. In the movie, Mason's first demand is to move everyone back 50 feet from the bank, but his ulterior motive was to buy time.

3. **Communication** – Effective negotiation requires clear, active listening and persuasive expression.

Miscommunication can quickly derail discussions. A common root cause of miscommunication is making incorrect assumptions. The solution to this is to ask pointed questions.

An assumption often made is that buyers always want a lower price. To achieve a middle-ground compromise, it is critical to listen to the wants and needs of the other party. You're specifically listening for interests and leverage. What do you want? What do they want? What might they be willing to give up? What are you willing to give up to?

Keep in mind that the amount of leverage a party has may dictate how far a compromise will go. It will not always result in a real bargain both parties will be happy with. If you can determine how desperately one side wants something, that "thing" will become the leverage.

During the movie, Mason's ability to communicate calmly and effectively with everyone was impressive, and Amelia was equally as skilled. There was a period when she was satisfied that they were releasing hostages on time and as promised, and this was buying the time he needed to figure a way out of the mess.

4. **Alternatives (BATNA)** – The *Best Alternative to a Negotiated Agreement (BATNA)* is what a party will do if no agreement is reached. If we do not get the initial desired results and no agreement is reached, our alternative will be to find another solution elsewhere. Having a strong BATNA gives a party more power at the table. This is the walkaway position.

In the ATM vestibule, Amelia suggests that this situation is not going to end well for Mason and his crew, and they should turn themselves in. Mason reminds her that his dad died in prison and would probably have chosen to die in a **"*hailstorm*"** of bullets instead. He suggests he would choose the hailstorm over prison if it came to that.

5. **Options** – Possible agreements or solutions that satisfy both parties' interests.

   Brainstorming and flexibility are key to generating useful options, as is determining any leverage you will have. Mason does find a creative solution *(which I won't specify here at the risk of major spoilers)* to satisfy everyone and avoid the hailstorm.

6. **Legitimacy** – Using fair standards, benchmarks, or norms to justify decisions.

   Legitimacy helps build trust and defend positions. Citing best-in-category solutions often can boost the perception of value. Amelia knew that Mason understood law enforcement protocols and would operate accordingly.

7. **Relationship** – To establish and maintain an ongoing connection between parties.

   In many negotiations, maintaining or improving the relationship is as important as the deal itself. Generally, people buy from people they know, like, and trust. If you feel like one vendor really isn't listening, is being overly pushy, and you get the sense that they used to be a slimy salesman, you may not be as motivated to give them your business.

   The rapport that Amelia and Mason demonstrated throughout the movie clearly made a huge difference in both the negotiation process and the outcome. Mason and his brother brilliantly navigated their relationship, as well. The importance of maintaining strong relationships with everyone connected to the negotiation—within your organization and external parties—shouldn't be underestimated.

AN EXAMPLE PROJECT

Let's say your CEO decides that she needs to put a reliable cell phone in the hands of every employee, so that they can communicate efficiently. And she tells you to make it happen. Let's see how you might use the seven categories discussed above to satisfy her request.

Your initial goal is to speak with a few cell phone vendors to see what kind of deal you can get, since you've never done this before.

1. **Interests:** In a follow-up conversation with your CEO to understand more about her specific goals, she reveals that she wants reliable cell phones to be distributed to everyone by year end, and she

has a line item in the budget to cover it. You confirm the number with the CFO, and of course, the CFO says he'd like you to come in well under that number. You plan to probe the cell phone vendors to see if they might be motivated by more than just selling at the highest price, such as increased market share or obtaining a referenceable client in your industry.

2. **Positions:** You need speed. The faster you get cell phones in the hands of your colleagues and have them communicating better, the more satisfied your CEO will be. The cheaper the deal, the happier your CFO will be. You don't know if the cell phone company representative has a quota and corresponding incentive to sell a certain number of phones in a specific time frame. This position knowledge would be beneficial to the overall negotiation. It's time to do some research and have some meetings to learn more.

3. **Communication:** You have a friendly conversation and discover that a top-tier cell phone vendor is eager to prove to his management team that he can make his quota by month end, is interested in obtaining a referenceable client in your industry, and offers volume pricing. But what else can they offer to sweeten the deal that will help you achieve your goals?

4. **Alternatives (BATNA)**: While of course there are other vendors, are there any other creative ways to satisfy the CEO's request? Instead of cell phones, you could acquire calling software for the computers everyone already has, plus an app for people who have personal cell phones.

5. **Options:** The seller has a quota to meet. Issuing a purchase order by the end of the month might help you gain additional concessions.

6. **Legitimacy:** Since there is volume pricing from one vendor, you can ask what the volume pricing policies are for all vendors and compare them.

7. **Relationship:** Through the course of speaking to references and meeting with several vendors, you sense who is highly professional, who is eager for your business, and whose product and service is rated as highly reliable.

So how will you get this deal done?

Perhaps you negotiate to start with a pilot group that includes the highest priority people in your company who need the phones and will serve as *"superusers"* for their teams.

You issue a small purchase order *(PO)* for 10% of the total number of cell phones you will need if the pilot goes well, at full price, for the pilot group. The vendor is excited to show their management team both the PO and the potential volume-discounted sale. Since you paid full price for the first 10%, they add, at no cost, a training and support program for your superusers, because they have a stake in ensuring there is positive feedback from this group.

In 30-days after receiving the phones and training, the superusers will be required to provide feedback that you and the vendor will review together. You've promised that positive feedback can be leveraged by the vendor for marketing, and assuming everything goes well, you will offer to be a reference to confirm your company's positive experience.

Meanwhile, your CEO is thrilled about seeing progress and results sooner than expected with this high priority group, and your pioneering people who are part of the pilot program will feel fully supported with hands-on training and support when they need it.

If the pilot doesn't go as well as everyone hopes, the vendor will have the chance to adjust their approach, or you can go to a different vendor without having spent all of your budget.

Sounds like a win-win-win, for your company, for the vendor, and for you, which is always the best outcome.

📢 DIRECTOR'S COMMENTS

The most prevailing myth of negotiations is the belief that anyone can do it without training and experience. There is a wide-ranging variety of knowledge required to be able to negotiate effectively. The art is understanding where you stand in the process and who wants to succeed more. Also relevant is the personal connection between the two parties, the size of the negotiation team, and the skills involved.

The overall key to a successful transaction is to listen to the other party's needs and offer compromises to accomplish the goal to completion.

My personal experience is that I've only met a handful of people who can negotiate effectively. In the movie, Mason's ability to quickly assess the situation and implement solutions to satisfy short and long term goals is exemplary.

Since negotiation is such a major part of Projectland, it is a skill well worth learning, and in fact is useful in everyday situations as well.

🎬 REALITY SHOW: WHEN LIFE IMITATES ART

In a real-life example of a tough negotiation, the CFO came to me and said, *"This transaction is costing us millions, and the seller won't budge with terms or pricing."* He then assigned me to negotiate the contract for a large software enterprise system, and clearly it wasn't going to be easy.

I learned that the seller had a great deal of leverage due to its unique position in the market. However, they were not the only good option for us, so I decided to make our point of view clear. I told one of their top executives, *"Your product is mediocre on a good day, your service is bad, and the price is high."* All of these things were true, but the vendor knew that they were the preferred software solution given our existing environment.

I had to employ all seven of the elements presented above.

As the buying negotiator, I did use certain leverage points just like in our hypothetical cell phone example. I discovered key hidden needs of the opposing party, such as a desire for future recommendations to other prospective customers and greater market share. This positioning was crucial. This valuable benefit to them was discussed at length and as a result, I was able to obtain better warranties and additional services for my company. Unfortunately, this negotiation took almost a year to complete, but all parties were satisfied in the end.

Our ability to explore all the needs of both parties and find out-of-the-box solutions to make everyone happy with the transaction was the key to success in this situation.

That's exactly what Mason did in *Cash Out*, too. I don't want to give away the ending in case you haven't seen the movie, but I found it to be very clever and a great example of an out-of-the-box solution that made everyone happy. Well, except for Amelia's boss at the FBI.

🎬 "IT'S A WRAP!"

In the world of projects, there always seem to be constraints or expectations related to time, budget, scope, quality, and stakeholder satisfaction.

This means that you will likely find yourself negotiating tradeoffs. This could be with executives, vendors, or team members.

When working to move the needle toward the overall goal, you may need to renegotiate the schedule. Likewise, you may need to give up some of the more elaborate and costly deliverables to meet budget and time goals. Always consider the other side's situation. This is useful for evaluating whether any creative measures can be applied in the pursuit of a compromise or solution.

When you keep the seven elements of negotiating like a pro in mind, you will be more likely to achieve a win-win.

PRESENTED BY...

JOHN SALAH, MBA

John is a seasoned procurement professional from the technology industry with advanced skills in negotiations and overall project management. He currently shares his expertise teaching business courses at a local college.

His distinguished career began over 40 years ago in Silicon Valley, spanning both large and small companies across diverse technology sectors, including entrepreneurial positions that showcase his versatility and vision. John has delivered results for companies specializing in hardware, software, and semiconductors, with notable tenures at industry giants including HP, Xilinx, McAfee, and others.

In his early career, John played a pivotal role at a computer and cell phone distributor in Northern California during the dawn of mobile technology. His first cell phone was part of GTE (now Verizon), making him cell number 42 in the San Francisco Bay Area—a testament to his position at the forefront of technological innovation.

Beginning his career in marketing, John strategically transitioned into Procurement, where he demonstrated exceptional leadership managing massive budgets *(e.g., airline and hotel expenditures exceeding $50 million)*. His expertise extends beyond corporate excellence into civic leadership, having been actively involved in city leadership groups and local government for the past three decades.

A Northern California resident for 50 years, John is the proud father of two adult daughters. His wife is impatiently awaiting grandchildren.

CHAPTER 22

CHECK YOUR SIX!

Maintaining Team Performance Under Pressure *(Top Gun)*

TOP GUN (1986)
Logline: "The Top Gun Naval Fighter Weapons School is where the best of the best train to refine their elite flying skills. When hotshot fighter pilot Maverick is sent to the school, his reckless attitude and cocky demeanor put him at odds with the other pilots, especially the cool and collected Iceman."[29]

SETTING THE SCENE

PETE MITCHELL *(TOM CRUISE)*, KNOWN BY HIS CALLSIGN, MAVerick, is a talented fighter pilot, but brash, unpredictable, and self-centered. He and his crewman, Radar Intercept Officer *(RIO)* Goose *(Anthony Edwards)*, are selected to attend the elite **"Top Gun Naval Fighter Weapons School"** *(Top Gun)* where their skills will be tested and their egos called into check.

Maverick gets his butt kicked in the first training flight. In the next, he teams up with Goose against their rival, Tom **"Iceman"** Kazansky, and Maverick's recklessness causes his own engines to flame out. This leads to perhaps the film's most emotional scene, in which Goose gets killed when the jet Maverick is piloting goes out of control.

Some pilots who graduate Top Gun are given surprise orders to fly on a top-secret mission to someplace exotic to fight against a shadowy country. We don't know the details. What we do know is that three crews ship out immediately after training.

> **HOT TAKE:** A gameplan is a necessity for any project to be successful. But when the situation is uncertain, complex, or untested, team members need to communicate with each other often, deliberately, and unambiguously.

 THE MOVIE MOMENT

Training is over, and Iceman *(Val Kilmer)*, Hollywood *(Whip Hubley)*, Maverick, and their RIOs are aboard an aircraft carrier, and her sister ship is disabled. She is in a foreign territory and the mission is air support for her rescue.

Here is what the team knows about the situation: They know there are enemy Mikoyan-Gurevich *(MiG)* fighter jets in the area. They know that the rules of engagement allow the team to return fire if the enemy makes a hostile act. Lastly, they know that the enemy has an anti-ship missile. This means the team must not only protect themselves, but they also must protect their carrier and the rest of the ships in the battle group.

The team is seeking two mission outcomes: support the rescue mission and keep the MiGs from getting within 100 miles of the aircraft carrier. The situation is both *complicated* and *complex*. It is complicated because it has a lot of moving parts with a lot going on. But, it should be predictable, especially because the fighter crews had just spent months at Top Gun working together as a team. They can't account for the enemy, however, making the situation *complex* as well. They don't necessarily know how the enemy will act or how to interpret any specific moves they make. Between the spectrum of options from the desirable *"responding systematically"* to the uncomfortable position of *"reacting quickly,"* the team is closer to reacting.

The famous aerial *"dogfight"* scene begins with Iceman and Hollywood launching their jets and heading to engage the enemy. Maverick is waiting on the flight deck as a reserve to take off within moments if needed.

"Two Bogeys! ......Four!.......No, FIVE Bogeys!"

Initial intelligence from the air controller is that there are two enemy aircraft. When the RIOs look more closely with their radars they discover two more, and then, after becoming even more deeply committed to the fight, they discover a fifth enemy aircraft!

This scene shows how complexity can alter circumstances in a very short time. Even in a whirlwind of activity, the entire team—that is, airborne crew, Maverick on deck, and air support— learn quickly and unambiguously the changing situation. Those closest to the problem, the RIOs with their radars, explicitly state the WHAT of the situation. And those farther away have the good sense to listen and not cloud the building picture with conjecture or speculation over the airwaves.

When I watch this scene, I listen closely to WHO is speaking and WHAT they are saying. And while there is a lot of activity taking place, I think about how much information is conveyed in the words that are spoken. This is information-rich dialogue, and it is succinct, clear, and unambiguous. This helps keep the entire team on the same page in a fast-changing environment.

But knowing the situation is useless unless action is taken!

Both teams engage each other in aerial combat, and soon Hollywood and his RIO are shot down. Team USA is now down by one plane. *(Again, even this emotional situation is communicated clearly and unambiguously to everyone.).* The audience feels a serious sense of urgency and anticipation. Air Combat Operations decides to launch Maverick to support Iceman who is now on his own. Will he make it in time to support Iceman and accomplish the mission? Because Maverick has been listening to the communications all along, he is quickly able to join the fight and locate one of the targets. He gets a good lock with his missile, and he fires.

Complexity strikes again when we learn that the catapults on the aircraft carrier are now broken and the airborne team is now completely on their own.

In the meantime, Iceman is nearby in a defensive position with a MiG on his tail. There is a LOT of airmanship taking place, but the radios are silent except for the communication that matters. As each pilot battles their enemy, they update the team on status. Each pilot has their own perspective but expands their overall understanding of the situation by listening. Each pilot is also willing to take direction from others, knowing that individual people on their team may have a better vantage point. This ability to take direction from others and change their own personal gameplan at a moment's notice enables the team as a whole to succeed.

As an example, Maverick regularly updates his team on his actions. He has always been a little erratic, but his quick thinking and immediate readiness for change is what they need to survive. Maverick shoots his missile and breaks left. He communicates this and articulates a plan on the radio. **"On the count of three, break hard right!"** Does everyone agree with that plan? Probably not. Is there time to worry about it? No! There's no time at all! Any plan that everyone understands is better than no plan when moments matter. By providing decisive direction, Maverick coordinates the team so they each focus on the right thing at that moment.

The team defeats the enemy force who ultimately departs and heads for home. Mission accomplished!

"ACTION!!!" PROJECTLAND SUCCESS TIPS

"Top Gun," at its heart, is a movie about personal growth, leadership, and team dynamics.

This blockbuster documents the character development of a highly talented fighter pilot as he learns—through painful experience—how to be less of a 'maverick' and more of a team player. Along the way, his fellow naval aviators improve their performance as a team, winning a life-or-death mission for their unit.

LEADERSHIP IN A FLEXIBLE ENVIRONMENT

Today there's a clear trend in Projectland toward flexibility. While changes in project management methods are obvious, I see the sheer proliferation of technology tools, apps, and frameworks as the biggest challenge. My last few projects all relied heavily on connecting new, innovative systems to established ones in new ways. And while most of these systems advertised that they would work *"seamlessly"* with whatever tech was already in place, in many cases the solution was much more complicated than advertised.

Today's corporate landscape is becoming more complicated and complex. Complicated situations may have many moving parts, but at least they are predictable…if you understand how it all works. Complexity raises its head by causing uncertainty, inserting risk, and making it difficult to effectively and efficiently achieve desired outcomes.

The world of Naval Aviation, specifically flying fighter jets off aircraft carriers, is both complicated and complex. Launching and recovering jets in the middle of the ocean with very little runway requires hundreds of aircrew, flight support, and deck crews to know, understand, and be proficient at their jobs.

A well-defined team can maximize the effectiveness of their resources *(knowledge, skills, and material)* by communicating clearly and unambiguously. Military teams, as demonstrated in the movie, do that, and you can too, no matter what role you play on a project. Know your mission, start with a plan, and communicate changing conditions succinctly and clearly. Let's break these practical tips down.

KNOW YOUR MISSION

Any military operation must have a mission. The mission is the entire reason the operation is needed in the first place. In corporations, I've typically heard this called the *"desired outcome."* Teams need to able to answer questions such as: How good is good enough, and what are our limitations *(or constraints)*?

START WITH A PLAN

Nineteenth century military theorist, Carl von Clausewitz, famously said that no plan survives first contact with the enemy. Sure, there have always been projects *(and missions!)* that get derailed right out of the station. But I trust that any fighter pilot will tell you that there is no better success factor than having the aircrew and team working together on plans and what-ifs in the intelligence center days and hours before the flight. Preparation gives the team the ability to flex effectively as circumstances change.

COMMUNICATE CHANGING CONDITIONS SUCCINCTLY AND CLEARLY

High-performing teams communicate with one another often, but also deliberately. Diving deep and getting granular are certainly needed in project work, especially in situations that are highly technical and complex. However, the successful team manages their dialog to match the situation and desired outcomes.

If the team needs to know about something, ensure they learn what they need to know, when they need to know it. Then, go a step further to make sure they understand what's happening and its impact to their work.

Speak clearly. Speak succinctly.

📣 DIRECTOR'S COMMENTS

As a young naval officer entering flight school, I knew there would be a lot on the menu: aerodynamics, weather, air operations, aircraft systems, and, of course, flying skills. What was a surprise to me—and challenge!—was the amount of time spent on communications. Communicating with air traffic control *(ATC)* is the obvious scenario. There are plenty of examples of ATC directing pilots in order to ensure safe and expeditious travel.

As an F-14 Tomcat Radar Intercept Officer *(RIO)*—a lot like Goose in Top Gun—I regularly monitored four or more radios during combat flights. The types of comms taking place would include command and control from the *"eye in the sky,"* coordination with your wingman, coordination with the overall strike force *(30+ aircraft)*, and communication with the aerial refueling tanker. *(Thank you, Texaco!)*

We RIOs were measured on communications proficiency. This was our ability to convey the most amount of information in the least amount of words or *"air time."* The best communicators are succinct and unambiguous.

Fast forward to when I was a flight instructor, and I noticed that the most common problem young aviators had with comms was ***"diarrhea of the mouth."*** When faced with trying to fly the aircraft, navigate a complicated airfield, and deal with the stress of being graded by the instructor, a young pilot would often make long-winded and rambling calls to ATC. Here's an example: ***"Tower, we want to land and take-off, then practice a no-flap approach, then fly around the visual pattern again before we come into land."*** That transmission might take fifteen seconds or so, and even then, the tower controller might not completely understand what the pilot requested.

However, the experienced tower controller who dealt with young students regularly, would respond back: ***"So you want two touch-and-goes then full-stop?"*** To which the exasperated student would reply, ***"Affirmative."*** The inexperienced, overwhelmed student reverted to giving too much extraneous detail.

As an instructor, I would regularly advise students to ***"speak with nouns only, no verbs"***. This is because the verbs were usually assumed. After twenty years in business, I realize now that what I was doing was telling them to concentrate on the WHAT, not the HOW.

When solving problems, HOW we do so is certainly important. However, the team can become confused when it doesn't clearly know WHAT the situation or limitation is.

Once they understand WHAT is expected, a team can figure out how to get there. In business today, people don't want to be told how to do something. Especially when working with skilled, experienced people, they tend to want to understand WHAT it is you want from them, and they want to figure out the optimal way to get there themselves.

🎬 REALITY SHOW: WHEN LIFE IMITATES ART

I recently led the rollout of a learning management system in a technically complex environment—this was our *"mission."* Normally, moving a tested application into production is straightforward: a simple *"cut-and-paste"* transfer. But in this case, the system's many moving parts—and undocumented elements—made the process both complicated and complex. Some pieces had to be rebuilt and tested directly in the live environment, which created real risks. Testing in the live system tends to be a major no-fly zone, because of the risk involved in impacting business functions reliant on that system.

Our team mapped four possible approaches, each with tradeoffs, and selected the one that best balanced risk and feasibility. The plan required migrating the application, connecting new data sources, moving hundreds of training files, and rebuilding critical functions.

When execution began, unexpected issues arose. For example, only part of the rule set transferred correctly. Because we had anticipated problems, the technical lead immediately flagged the issue, proposed a workaround, and the team quickly adjusted. To minimize delays, feedback during execution was concise and focused, quite different from extensive planning discussions.

We encountered several more surprises, but by keeping communication clear and reducing unnecessary *"noise,"* we managed them effectively. The lesson was simple but vital: in complex projects, success depends less on perfect planning than on disciplined communication and adaptive teamwork under changing conditions.

It's natural for individual team members to want to move their work ahead as quickly as possible. However, experienced project people know that details matter, and taking a moment to communicate clearly and succinctly can make the difference between success and failure.

🎬 "IT'S A WRAP!"

High-performing teams communicate with each other at the right level for the situation. I hope you can take these examples of communications in complicated and complex situations back to your own teams to improve your performance. In most cases, we all *(me included)* probably talk a little too much!

🎬 PRESENTED BY...

DAVE LOZINGER

Dave Lozinger is a management consultant, specializing in program management and human performance. For the last twenty years he has helped clients systematically understand and execute their work by establishing clear outcomes, processes, responsibilities, and decision-making.

He has broad experience in multiple industries and business functions, including energy, pharmaceuticals, retail, engineering, and transportation. Dave's biggest professional accomplishment is having led the project management and change management of a short-notice effort to greatly improve performance of a $1.7B business planning cycle that had already started. Dave is privileged to have served and consulted with clients like ITT Exelis, Chevron, Merck, Norfolk Southern, Best Buy, and more.

Prior to entering Corporate America, Dave completed two carrier-based deployments as a US Naval Flight Officer, flying the F-14 Tomcat. He finished his career as a flight instructor where he trained US Navy and Air Force flight officers, as well as those in the Royal Saudi Air Force, German Luftwaffe, and Singaporean Navy. Dave's most meaningful military accomplishment was being awarded Instructor of the Year over 75 others.

He graduated from the US Naval Academy with a degree in Physics.

Dave and his bride live in eastern Pennsylvania, where they are raising the last two of their five kids.

ACKNOWLEDGEMENTS

FIRST AND FOREMOST, DAWN AND JERRY WOULD LIKE TO THANK our wonderful team of contributors for sharing their wisdom, time, and passion for film. This was a collective effort if there ever was one.

Extra special appreciation goes to Sheila Shah and Victory Oghenovo for providing positive peer reviews that helped to strengthen chapters for readers, as well as cheer our authors onward.

Many rounds of applause go to the authors who also doubled as peer reviewers *(in order of screen time)*: Rachel Mussell, Tanya Boyd, Michael Schafer, Bruno Morgante, Justus Aiyela, Dr. Mike Clayton, Rosalin Walcott, Jesse Middaugh, and Joe Pusz. Teamwork indeed makes the dream work!

Thanks also to our incredible cover artist and interior designer *(of the book, not our homes)*, Kerry Ellis, who never fails to amaze us with her creativity and dedication to excellence.

To our talented team behind the scenes, thank you **"Butterfly Beth"** Montgomery and Luis Vivar for your creativity, encouragement, and launch support.

Many thanks to Ugla Hauksdóttir, award-winning director of *The Fires* for fact-checking her father's chapter for accuracy. We can't wait for *The Fires* to come to theaters near all of us and wish you continued great success in the movie business.

To our families and friends, thank you for sharing movie nights, enduring frustrated word wrestling matches, and generously giving up your time while we typed through weekends and late-night double features.

Special thanks from Jerry to Sharon and Elizabeth Manas for putting up with endless marathon meetings with Dawn, and to Mike Reindel—the unsung hero keeping Dawn sane, ever the willing popcorn companion, and our resident Lord of the Rings fact checker.

Finally, we'd like to thank the filmmakers, screenwriters, and actors of the world, who inspire us with their vision and talent. And, of course, the Academy.

SPECIAL NOTE FROM THE EDITORS

THANK YOU SO MUCH FOR READING *PROJECTLAND GOES TO the Movies*! If you've enjoyed this book, please consider taking a few moments to post a short review on the retailer of your choice. We would greatly appreciate it, and your honest review may help other project people discover the book.

Please consider this your personal VIP invitation to join us and our project gurus in Projectland on your favorite social platform and/or at an upcoming event in the virtual or real world.

The best way to join us and be notified of upcoming learning opportunities *(many of which are free)* is to subscribe to our newsletter at PMOtraining.com.

Creating a book is a labor of love, and this book was especially so. We enjoyed collaborating with so many experts from around the world to bring their perspectives to the page in a way that we hope you found entertaining and helpful.

On behalf of all of us authors, peer reviewers, and movie buffs we wish you all the best in Projectland and beyond!

With gratitude,
Dawn & Jerry

CONTINUE YOUR PROJECTLAND JOURNEY!

MEET THE PLAYERS IN PROJECTLAND:
DECIDE THE RIGHT PROJECT ROLES & GET PEOPLE ON BOARD

THROUGH CLEVER ANIMAL AVATARS AND COLORFUL STORIES, gain practical insights about navigating the mysterious people side of projects.

Get your complimentary sample at ProjectGuruPress.com or get your copy at your favorite bookseller.

ENDNOTES

1. *IMDb, "Moneyball (2011),"* Accessed September 1, 2025, https://www.imdb.com/title/tt1210166/

2. *IMDb, "V for Vendetta (2005),"* Accessed September 1, 2025, https://www.imdb.com/title/tt0434409/

3. *IMDb, "The Great Escape (1963),"* Accessed September 1, 2025, https://www.imdb.com/title/tt0057115/

4. *IMDb, "Ocean's 11 (2001),"* Accessed September 1, 2025, https://www.imdb.com/title/tt0240772/

5. *IMDb, "Fantozzi (1975),"* Accessed September 1, 2025, https://www.imdb.com/title/tt0071486/

6. *IMDb, "Star Wars: Episode V – The Empire Strike Back (1980),"* Accessed September 1, 2025, https://www.imdb.com/title/tt0080684/

7. *IMDb, "Ghostbusters (1984),"* Accessed September 1, 2025, https://www.imdb.com/title/tt0087332/

8. *IMDb, "The Martian (2015),"* Accessed September 1, 2025, https://www.imdb.com/title/tt3659388/

9. *IMDb, "The Lord of the Rings: Fellowship of the Ring (2001),"* Accessed September 1, 2025, https://www.imdb.com/title/tt0120737/

10. *IMDb*, "12 Angry Men (1957)," Accessed September 1, 2025, https://www.imdb.com/title/tt0050083/

11. *IMDb*, "Wonder Woman (2017)," Accessed September 1, 2025, https://www.imdb.com/title/tt0451279/

12. https://www.cnbc.com/2023/12/21/harvard-professor-dont-fail-fast-fail-often-fail-intelligently.html?msockid=052a8b4596666b6114209d1d97c16a98, Accessed August 28, 2025

13. *IMDb*, "Aliens (1986)," Accessed September 1, 2025, https://www.imdb.com/title/tt0090605/

14. *IMDb*, "The Fires (2025)," Accessed September 1, 2025, https://www.imdb.com/title/tt31272500/

15. *IMDb*, "Apollo 13 (1995)," Accessed September 1, 2025, https://www.imdb.com/title/tt0112384/

16. *IMDb*, "The Italian Job (2003)," Accessed September 1, 2025, https://www.imdb.com/title/tt0317740/

17. Nick Hutchinson, *Rise of the Reader: Strategies For Mastering Your Reading Habits and Applying What You Learn* (The Reading Revolution Publishing, 2023).

18. *IMDb*, "The Man from Snowy River (1982)," Accessed September 1, 2025, https://www.imdb.com/title/tt0084296/

19. Ryan Holiday, *Ego is the Enemy* (Portfolio, 2016).

20. *IMDb*, "The Greatest Night in Pop (2024)," Accessed September 1, 2025, https://www.imdb.com/title/tt30796448/

21. https://usaforafrica.org/about-us/ accessed August 29, 2025

22. *A Note from Marcia Thomas, Executive Director*, https://usaforafrica.org/about-us/, accessed August 20, 2025.

23. Quote extracted from the video, "A Conversation with Lionel Ritchie" accessed August 30, 2025: https://usaforafrica.org/a-conversation-with-lionel-richie/

24. https://www.productplan.com/glossary/change-enablement/

25. *IMDb, "Raiders of the Lost Ark (1981)," Accessed September 1, 2025,* https://www.imdb.com/title/tt0082971/

26. *IMDb, "Jurassic Park (1993)," Accessed September 1, 2025,* https://www.imdb.com/title/tt0107290/

27. *IMDb, "School of Rock (2003)," Accessed September 1, 2025,* https://www.imdb.com/title/tt0332379/

28. *IMDb, "Cash Out (2024)," Accessed September 1, 2025,* https://www.imdb.com/title/tt24131288/

29. *IMDb, "Top Gun (1986)," Accessed September 1, 2025,* https://www.imdb.com/title/tt0092099/

www.ingramcontent.com/pod-product-compliance
Lightning Source LLC
Chambersburg PA
CBHW052029030426
42337CB00027B/4918